CONTENTED COWS
Still Give Better Milk

CONTENTED COWS

Still
Give Better Milk

The Plain Truth about Employee
Engagement and Your Bottom Line

BILL CATLETTE
RICHARD HADDEN

WILEY

John Wiley & Sons, Inc.

Published by John Wiley & Sons, Inc., Hoboken, New Jersey.
Published simultaneously in Canada.

For general information on our other products and services or for technical support, please contact our Customer Care Department within the United States at (800) 762-2974, outside the United States at (317) 572-3993 or fax (317) 572-4002.

Wiley publishes in a variety of print and electronic formats and by print-on-demand. Some material included with standard print versions of this book may not be included in e-books or in print-on-demand. If this book refers to media such as a CD or DVD that is not included in the version you purchased, you may download this material at http://booksupport.wiley.com. For more information about Wiley products, visit www.wiley.com.

ISBN 978-1-118-29273-0 (cloth); ISBN 978-1-118-33401-0 (ebk);
ISBN 978-1-118-33180-4 (ebk); ISBN 978-1-118-33510-9 (ebk)

Printed in the United States of America

10 9 8 7 6 5 4 3 2 1

To William Catlette, Bill's dad, who taught him a lifetime of lessons about determination, frugality, respect for others, having high standards, and how to fish. Only one of those "courses" was altogether fun, but they all made their mark. We miss him.

CONTENTS

ACKNOWLEDGMENTS

This book would not have been written at all were it not for an introduction made by Jeb Blount, of Sales Gravy, and the encouragement of Lauren Murphy, our acquisitions editor at John Wiley & Sons, Inc., or nearly as well without a lot of helpful wordsmithing by development editor Christine Moore. All three are consummate professionals, and we thoroughly enjoy working with them.

We are indebted to Brad Ziemba and Mark McCranie, who once again helped with the financial research associated with the Contented Cow companies. A very special shout out goes to Jermia Jerdine, a graduating senior at the University of Memphis who also holds a full-time job and still volunteered to assist us with research and number crunching. This young lady is going to go places.

Thanks, too, to the representatives of Plantronics Mexico, Marriott, Inception, and Zappos, whom we peppered with questions during our site visits, and to Joyce Folk of the Atlanta Airport Marriott Gateway, who served up career insights along with strong coffee and a mean plate of eggs. Through her gracious hospitality, Rebekah Stewart, owner of Brigadoon Lodge and Flyline Wine, helped make the writing venue quieter, more scenic, and enjoyable.

For their time on the phone and over e-mail, we thank those we talked to from Maple Leaf Sports and Entertainment, Bazaarvoice, Hanmer MSL, LaRosa's Restaurants, the City of Lakeway, Consolidated Health Systems, Dow Chemical, and Chick-fil-A. You brought to life for us what it means to be a distinguished workplace.

We are eternally thankful to the folks at Nestlé for their support, without which this book would have a very different title.

We are grateful to our spouses for their unflinching support; no, it's more than that—for putting up with our single-minded obsession with this project for better than three months. Christine, Mary, we're fortunate to have you in our lives.

How Do the Best Get Better?

The task of leadership is not to put greatness into people, but to elicit it, for the greatness is there already.

—John Buchan

Since the original publication of this book in 1998, the workspace—indeed, much of the world—has been stood on its head. Oh, people (most of us, anyhow) still have jobs that produce income that allows us to sustain ourselves. But nearly all the terms of the deal have changed.

The old Protestant work ethic to which our parents and grandparents subscribed—the maxim that suggested that good things will happen to you if you keep your nose to the grindstone and your mouth closed—busted. The notion that, by definition, all work occurs within the confines of an employer's workplace—gone. Loyalty and obedience to the organization—vamoose, along with job security and defined pension benefits. The bright line between personal and professional time and activities—completely blurred. The assumption that there must be something wrong with you if you are unemployed for more than a few weeks—forget it. The expectation that workers would receive training before starting a new job function—outsourced, eliminated, or relegated to do-it-yourself status.

In a nutshell, the game has changed in material ways. The rules are different, the field is bigger, the pace exponentially quicker, the goalposts narrower, shareholders less forgiving, and the talent is more elusive, cynical, and mercenary. An entire project or career can be launched or terminated with 138 characters and an RT.

One aspect of workspace physics remains rock solid, however: the precept that focused, fully engaged workers produce more and better stuff, yielding better outcomes. Motivated people move faster; they always have and always will. When you view this through the *other* end of the telescope, it is obvious that no one—repeat, no one—despite repeated attempts by a number of commercial airlines, can achieve success by foisting disgruntled, disenfranchised workers upon paying customers. It's a simple, relatively understood and accepted concept—at least in *theory*.

It's another thing altogether in practice, however. We tend to lose sight of what motivates people to want to contribute more, become weak-kneed at the prospect of actually *doing* those things, or arrogantly (and mistakenly) conclude that a weak labor market overrides the need to be concerned about them.

Our purpose is to once again bring front and center the very real, tangible benefits of treating people right in the workplace and to clearly define just what "right" means. (*Hint:* It may not be what you think.)

How does one organization achieve unprecedented levels of success over a substantial period of time while a nearly identical competitor struggles—or goes down the tubes completely? Is the former's success the result of better mousetraps, dumb luck, or maybe just better execution? Consider, for example:

- How Google could blow right past Microsoft, Yahoo!, and Baidu to totally dominate the search space with greater than 80 percent market share.
- How 150-year-old General Mills continues to capture an ever-greater share of supermarket shelf space and your kitchen cupboard with brands such as Progresso, Bisquick, Wheaties, and Pillsbury.

- And will somebody please explain how it can be that North Carolina–based Nucor Steel is able to operate a $20 billion business (one of the largest steel companies on earth) with a headquarters staff of fewer than 100 people—and do it in one of the worst economies in a century—*without* laying people off?

In each of the aforementioned cases, and in every similar success story we have been able to find, managements are taking strikingly similar approaches. Our mission is to discover, chronicle, and help others replicate those approaches. As Thomas Edison said, "There is a better way. . . . Find it!"

Discretionary Effort—Nobody Has Moved the Cheese

Not much has changed about human nature since psychologist Elton Mayo first studied the relationship between motivation and productivity at the Hawthorne Works of the Western Electric Company in the late 1920s—and that was more than 90 years ago!

In a series of motivational experiments titled the *Harvard Hawthorne Studies*, Mayo—using a real company, real managers, and real employees—first uncovered the unmistakable relationship between worker attitudes and production, or output. Essentially, he learned two things:

1. Human beings are uniquely capable of *regulating their involvement* in and commitment to a given task or endeavor.
2. The extent to which we do or do not fully contribute is governed *more by attitude* than by necessity, fear, or economic influence.

In a nutshell, what Mayo learned—which has been reinforced by a number of subsequent experiments and surveys—is that there is an increment of human effort that individuals can apply exclusively at their discretion. This finding led to the coining of the term *discretionary effort* (DE), which is defined as the difference between that minimally necessary level of effort and that which we can, in fact, achieve. In short, it represents the distinction between obedience and high performance and between those who are managed versus those who are led. Its expenditure is clearly (and completely) a matter of choice. In the workspace, it is the difference between the minimum level of effort that employees must expend to keep their jobs and that of which they are truly capable. The equation therefore is:

Personal Capability − Minimum Requirements = Discretionary Effort

The context within which Mayo discovered DE at Western Electric was one in which employees were withholding it, for a variety of reasons. They were consciously performing at only a minimally satisfactory level, or, as some might put it, they kept showing up at work (and getting paid) even though they were essentially on strike.

Unfortunately, not much has changed. The only difference between then and now is that workers withheld discretionary effort much more covertly back then. People are open about it today, because the stick— the punishment for lack of effort, as in "carrot and stick"—has absolutely been worn out and thus has little effect. Moreover, it is relatively easy to sleep through meetings with your eyes open and make shopping on eBay or playing Cow Clicker look like work.

It's Your People, Stupid

As Richard Pascale of the Stanford Graduate School of Business put it, "The trouble is, 99 percent of managerial attention today is devoted to the techniques that squeeze more out of the existing paradigm—and it's killing us. Tools, techniques, and 'how-to' recipes won't do the job without a higher order . . . concept of management."

As managers career wildly from one tool or tactic to another, many lose sight of the fact that the critical difference between a brilliant strategy and one that gets successfully executed resides in the hearts and minds of people—specifically, the members of your workforce. We can scream, exhort, and rattle the saber all we want, but we'll never achieve successful organizational change without their willing participation.

In many cases, establishing alternative precepts (or the "higher order" as Pascale puts it) flies dead in the face of a definition of the managerial role that's been held and nurtured for literally hundreds of years—namely, the old, authoritarian, "plantation mentality" scenario that features the manager as "order giver" and the employee as "order taker."

This failure to change our outlook toward the management of human effort has become the chief impediment to competitiveness for many, both here and elsewhere. We certainly don't lack the brains, ability, or technology. Rather, it's a matter of will, specifically the will to change. Some have it, and some haven't gotten there yet.

Our purpose is to entice those in the latter category to move along by calling attention to a few organizations that do "get it"—while highlighting the very real, hard, bottom-line impact they (and their shareholders) are enjoying as a result.

The Premise

Just the Facts

Everyone is entitled to his own opinion, but no one is entitled to his own set of facts.

—James Schlesinger

Every year, respected business publications like *Fortune, INC*, and Bloomberg *BusinessWeek* rank (in seemingly endless ways) those companies that are doing the best job in their chosen industry or niche. We read about the "Most Admired" and "Most Innovative," the "Customer Service Champs," the ones generating the "Highest Shareholder Return," the "Fastest Growing," the XYZ 500, and the list goes on.

We can't help but notice that in this blizzard of rankings and ratings the same organizations seem to take home the trophies year after year—companies such as Coca-Cola, Disney, Google, Southwest Airlines, Intel, and Procter & Gamble. We certainly don't think that the frequency of their presence has anything to do with shortcuts that writers or editors of these publications take. No, there's something else at work.

Outside the corporate boardroom, but certainly no less engaged in the world of business, lies the arena of professional sports. Here, too, there is a fairly short list of perennial overachiever teams such as the Boston Celtics, New England Patriots, and Chicago Cubs.

You're still thinking about that last name, aren't you? We were just checking to see if you're awake. We can still hope for the Cubbies, though, right?

What we find among persistent winners in just about any labor-intensive endeavor is that an extremely high ratio of them also happens to have adopted leadership habits that make the organization a great place to work—not an *easy* place to work, but a very good one. Our passion has been to study many of these firms over the past three decades, and it's been our pleasure to work with a few of them up close and personal. It is truly impressive to encounter a workplace where people are hitting on all cylinders—whether your vantage point is that of an insider, a customer, or as we're about to prove yet again, a shareholder.

Since 1982, *Fortune* magazine has published an annual listing of what it calls the "Most Admired Corporations," a ranking—overall and by industry—of those organizations with the best business reputations. It is now produced in both domestic U.S. and global versions. Corporate executives, outside directors, and financial analysts judge companies according to the following criteria:

- Product quality
- Global competitiveness
- Value as a long-term investment
- Use of corporate assets

- Financial soundness
- Innovation
- Social responsibility
- People management

The top 15 companies on the 2012 "Global Most Admired" list are Apple, Google, Amazon.com, Coca-Cola, IBM, Federal Express, Berkshire Hathaway, Starbucks, Procter & Gamble, Southwest Airlines, McDonald's, Johnson & Johnson, Disney, BMW, and General Electric.

A reasonably astute observer might suggest that this list consists of some of the best brands on earth, and it does.

Likewise, it would be fair to say that nearly all of the companies atop this list also happen to be regarded as truly exceptional places to work. In fact, 13 of them have also been formally recognized (most of them more than once) as one of the very best places to work by *Fortune*, Glassdoor, *BusinessWeek*, or comparable rating media. Similarly, none of the firms regarded as best places to work shows up in (or anywhere near) the bottom 50 on Fortune's "Most Admired" list. Rather, some of the companies at the bottom of that list are also regarded as especially *unattractive* places to work.

As more than casual observers of these relationships for better than 15 years (indeed the first version of this book cited the comparison in 1998), we can affirm that this finding is anything but an aberration.

Yet, being selected onto lists of this sort involves a fair amount of subjective judgment, even when that judgment considers the opinions of large numbers of one's peers. Hence, we've made it a point to analyze further by looking for consistency in an organization's record. We also examine "harder" data, such as financial performance comparisons between those firms with great workplace reputations relative to benchmarked norms.

Here again, the conclusions are clear: those publicly held firms with good workplace reputations tend to outperform both their immediate peers and aggregate financial benchmarks on a long-term basis— something that's proved true in both "down" and "up" economic cycles. As a case in point, during the period 1997–2010, which included two up and two down cycles, the publicly held "100 Best Companies to Work For" outperformed both the S&P 500 and the Russell 3000 benchmark indices by a 4:1 margin.

> *Take away my factories, and I will build a new and better factory; but take away my people, and grass will grow on the factory floor.*
> —Andrew Carnegie

In the first edition of this book in 1998, we identified six companies, (the Contented Cows), that enjoyed well-earned reputations as employers of choice. We paired them with six competitors that didn't have quite the same workplace reputation (the Common Cows). We conducted a rigorous comparison of their sales growth, earnings, productivity, and return to shareholders over a 10-year period (1986–1995). The Contented Cows outgrew, outearned, and in general, outperformed the Common Cows by a substantial margin.

After the book was published, we extended the comparison period to test the results by including the impact of the 2000 recession and found that the advantages of the Contented Cows became even more compelling. Over the 15-year comparison period, the Contented Cows outgrew their counterparts by a 10:1 margin, outearned them by $111 billion, generated 16 times as much wealth for shareholders, and created tens of thousands more sustainable jobs.

To mollify those who might suggest that we had somehow managed to pick the right comparison companies and time period to advance our theory, we initiated an exercise whose outcome we couldn't control. Specifically, we challenged the management of the Fidelity Investments Magellan Fund to a 12-month head-to-head contest. The challenge was that our little mythical Contented Cows Mutual Fund—which consisted of publicly held employers of choice and was comanaged by a friend who had just obtained his broker's license—could go head to head with what was then the biggest mutual fund on the planet.

The odds of this being a fair fight were slim. Our offer was that Fidelity could make the rules and that the loser would donate $1,000 to the Cystic Fibrosis Foundation. After being ignored by Magellan fund manager Bob Stansky, we implemented the challenge unilaterally (after all, mutual funds report their Net Asset Values on a daily basis) and dutifully reported the comparative results every quarter on our ContentedCows .com website.

Do you know how it turned out? Of course, you do. (We're telling you about it, aren't we? Do you really think we'd be bringing it up if we lost?) The Contented Cows fund beat Magellan by 8.8 percent over the period—and to be good sports, we made the donation anyway.

So there you have it. Contented Cows really *do* give better milk.

Since then, we have travelled the globe advising corporate leadership teams and association management audiences about the very real, tangible benefits of treating people right. We've defined for them in vivid detail just what "right" means and offered straightforward, executable prescriptions for attaining those same results.

People have asked periodically if we thought it might be time to update the story. In general, we have resisted (okay, Bill has resisted), largely on the grounds that once you know that $2 + 2 = 4$, there is no need to continually reprove it. Moreover, the basic tenets of leadership are virtually timeless.

Yet we have realized after a decade of hearing this question—with the help of our editor, Lauren Murphy—that readers aren't so much interested in a rejustification of the Contented Cows axiom; instead, they are asking for some fresh examples and fresh stories, with maybe a little reaffirmation of the original premise. There is only so much you can hear about the Southwests and FedExes before you ask, "Is that all there is? Doesn't anybody *else* get these things right?"

Therein lies the challenge. Although each of us is an optimist, we are also realists. Practicality reminds us that for every company like Southwest Airlines that has proved in spades that a fired-up workforce is indeed a potent competitive weapon—and that paying customers shouldn't be locked in cramped spaces with grumpy employees—there are a thousand others who either fail to grasp the concept or lack the discipline to faithfully execute it. So although it's not exactly a search for a needle in a haystack, it can be difficult finding real, bona fide exemplars.

It wouldn't be as hard if you could just go to the lists of the annually announced best places to work and accept them at face value, but you can't. Rather, we won't, because there are more than a few organizations that have managed either to game the system in order to achieve recognition or have had the good fortune of a strong, short-lived tailwind. We're more interested in those that have demonstrated over a long period, through good times and bad, that credible leadership practices are deeply embedded in their business strategy. That is precisely why we've only now opted to include Google, a relative newcomer, on our list of Contented Cows.

Admittedly, there is a good deal of subjectivity involved in first defining what an employer of choice actually is. Serious consternation comes into play when determining which organizations legitimately qualify. We rely on essentially three sources to separate the Contented Cows from the rest of the herd:

1. Credible "best places to work" types of lists, such as Glassdoor's "Best Places to Work—Employees' Choice Awards," Bloomberg *BusinessWeek*'s "Best Places to Launch a Career," and *Fortune*

magazine's annual ranking of the "100 Best Companies to Work For," compiled by The Great Place to Work Institute.

2. Our colleagues in the Society for Human Resource Management, with whom we've consulted extensively on the subject.

3. Our own judgment based on 50-plus years of combined business experience. In the final analysis, we asked ourselves: "Is this a company that we would recommend to a good friend or family member who was looking for a job?"

One message we've gotten loud and clear from readers and others who have been kind enough to offer suggestions is that although you want to hear about more of the positive exemplars, you don't have a need to hear as much about comparison companies whose workplace reputations don't quite measure up. So we've taken a slightly different approach with this edition.

Specifically, we have doubled the complement of Contented Cows and in general benchmarked their performance against respected broader indices rather than individual industry peers.

As you can see from the list that follows, we have again incorporated organizations representing the broad spectrum of commerce, to include the manufacturing, service, and distribution sectors. There are two each from health care, technology, energy, and hospitality; three from the food world; and one from entertainment/media. Some are old, some new; some quite large, others smallish in size. Most operate internationally, and two of the firms are headquartered outside the United States. With the exception of employee-owned Publix, all are publicly held. In short, they are quite representative of the commercial landscape, and the broader market against which we have benchmarked them.

Although we've identified the 12 Contented Cow companies for the aforementioned reasons, we didn't limit our research to these organizations. We'll give examples throughout the following chapters that we've gleaned from personal experiences, site visits, and interviews with members of other organizations, some of which will no doubt be familiar to you. However, let us be clear: organizations that are considered a Contented Cow company must meet the following minimum criteria:

1. *Sustainability:* Have a business model and track record that signal they will be around for a while

2. *Continuity:* Have been in business for at least five years

3. *Desirability:* Are generally and demonstrably regarded by the people who work there as a good place to work, with positive, affirming, sensible, and affordable employment policies and practices

The Fine Print

Real (and lasting) success in business requires more than just enlightened employment practices. You must have market-worthy products or services, the ability to deliver them when and where the customer wants (at a price they're willing to pay), and, to be sure, capable leadership.

We also recognize that just as productive employees are not always satisfied, satisfied employees are not always productive. In fact, some may be satisfied because they *don't* have to be productive. And, of course, there are those who prefer to "check their brains" at the door and work only with their bodies (if at all). So we are not asking you to accept the notion that the *only* factor explaining the huge financial performance advantage of the Contented Cow companies happens to be their employment practices.

But we are asking you to consider that it's virtually impossible for any labor-intensive organization to get to (let alone stay at) the top without having adopted such practices. In an age when speed, flexibility, and flawless execution have become the primary markers for competitive advantage, human factors are mission critical. Indeed, within the culture of the successful organization, the identification of the employees themselves with the company mission, vision, and values is so great that it made sense to use the Contented Cow metaphor interchangeably for both corporate entity and its constituent parts—in other words, its people. We think the facts and figures you're about to see make the case in no uncertain terms.

Our current research led us to evaluate 10 years' worth of financial statements for literally dozens of companies. For comparison purposes, we settled on the period from 2001 to 2011 and chose financial measures that are statistically significant, universally available, and commonly understood. Sales and earnings data are generally portrayed for the 10-year period from 2001 to 2010, whereas stock data are generally portrayed for the period from 2002 to 2011, owing to its timelier reporting. Now that we have established the background and parameters, here is our list of comparison companies:

Contented Cows

Technology	Food	Health Care
Google	General Mills	Novo Nordisk
Qualcomm	J.M. Smucker	Roche
	Publix Super Markets	
Energy	**Hospitality**	**Entertainment/Media**
Chesapeake Energy	Marriott	The Walt Disney
NuStar Energy	Starbucks	Company

Now, before going any further, ask yourself this question: Based on what I know of these companies, which—if any—would I want to work for? In fact, while you're at it, why not make a list of your *own* comparison companies? That way, if you at all doubt our premise, you can check them out and see for yourself. Go ahead. (It's okay to write in the book; you paid for it.)

My List of Comparison Companies

1.

2.

3.

4.

5.

If you come up with some strong exemplars, you might also want to list two or three specific characteristics that make each organization a great place to work. Then, the next time a friend is job hunting and you get the inevitable "networking" call, steer your friend to one of the companies on the list. If you're willing to share, we'd like to hear about your discoveries as well.

It is fitting perhaps that the comparison period includes two economic recessions (2000 and 2007–2009) that bookend an interim period of modest economic growth. Businesses are truly tested during such periods. Anybody can make money when the sun is shining and the wind is at their back.

The Business Case

A middling economy notwithstanding, the Contented Cows indeed made money for themselves and their shareholders during the comparison period. Witness the facts that:

- The average annual total stock return for the Contented Cow companies (combined) during the period 2002–2011 was 10.7 percent, beating the broader market average by a whopping 9.7 percent annually, creating a wealth premium of approximately $70 billion annually.

- Every company's shareholder performance bested the S&P 500 for the period.

- Of the 12 companies' 10 year shareholder returns, 8 also beat their industry averages.

- During a period when the U.S. economy performed at a subpar level (real gross domestic product [GDP] growth in the nonrecession years of the 2000s averaged just 2.7 percent a year, versus a 3.3 percent average between 1947 and 2011), the Contented Cow companies averaged 23.4 percent annual revenue growth, far outpacing their peers and the broader market.

So once again, the Contented Cow companies have a nasty habit of growing faster, creating more wealth for shareholders, and creating more sustainable jobs. Game, set, match.

Where's the Beef?

The point is actually a simple one. So simple in fact that the Carnation Company, now part of Nestlé, may have put it best many years ago when they suggested that their condensed milk product came "From Contented Cows."

Any serious dairy farmer will tell you that for as long as they've milked cows, they've employed methods of care to produce healthier, more contented, and most important, higher-yielding cows. Animal science studies at respected universities suggest that dairy cattle that are named—and referred to by name (yes, you read that correctly)—and that enjoy the benefits of dry, level, amply-sized feed lot space produce upward of an additional 60 gallons of milk annually. At $3.75 per gallon, that works out to a little over $54 billion of potential annual benefit for the world's dairy farmers. Ten years at that rate, and you've got yourself a stimulus package.

In a similar vein, those organizations that can be consistently identified as winners in their respective fields—whether it's making raspberry jam or pharmaceuticals, delivering lattes or natural gas, or furnishing a home away from home to weary travelers—also happen to be known as some of the best places on earth to work. Unlike the age-old conundrum of the chicken and the egg, we don't think there is any doubt about which came first in these cases. Truly excellent organizations differentiate themselves from the start as employers of choice. This allows them to hire and retain top-drawer people, harvest their ideas and discretionary effort, and then distinguish their products and services in the marketplace. Think it's a coincidence? We don't.

We have a lot to say about what Contented Cow companies are doing, but perhaps just as notable is what they *aren't* doing. Unlike the approach that many of their competitors take, management in these companies is not betting the ranch that technology and capital spending alone will lead them to a more competitive posture. Nor do they focus their employee engagement and retention efforts on faddish tactics.

Please don't confuse contentment with complacency. The fact that a cow is contented in no way interferes with its inclination or ability to "jump over the moon." Instead, companies that follow the Contented Cow path seem to agree with the idea—well expressed by former Procter & Gamble chairman and chief executive officer Owen (Brad) Butler—that "productivity comes from people, not machines."

Let's also establish, early on, that leadership is not about getting to the "smiley face." Even when done well, it can be difficult, demanding, and unpleasant, resulting in bumps and bruises. Life, after all, is a contact sport, and leadership is about close-quarters contact.

Jim Barksdale, my* former boss at FedEx, was fond of saying, "We're in business for exactly one reason, to get and keep customers." To the extent that an organization is at all labor-dependent, we propose that the principal requirement for operationalizing that aim is the creation of a satisfied, fully engaged workforce.

For many years, we have stayed at Marriott hotels just about every week. Although the ubiquity of their properties, indeed, has something to do with that decision, we mainly continue to stay with them because their employees are nice, are polite, and perform. I'm sure they've got a few grumpy people somewhere, but they must be hiding them in the basement on the third shift, because I've yet to run into one of them. Throughout his long career, Bill Marriott consistently commented on the critical nature of staff members' attitudes in his business.

The truth is that most of our products and services, technologies, methods, tools, and strategies can all be copied. However, it's not as easy to duplicate a focused, caring workforce. In the final analysis, "people factors" are frequently the key source of competitive advantage—the factor least visible to the naked eye and most difficult to emulate. We simply must accept that most businesses aren't so much capital, expertise, or even product-driven as they are *people*-driven.

Clearly, this hasn't always been the case. Under the earliest business model, the corporation was little more than tangible property—at first a piece of real estate (e.g., a farm) and later a factory. Then over time it became the financiers—those who had supplied the capital necessary to expand and automate the farm or factory—who emerged as the primary centers of influence. But as the very nature of "work" continues to evolve and disaggregate, its focus shifts more to knowledge, service, and speed, hence the significance and ownership of the "hard assets" diminishes.

Authors' note: Assuming the reader to be indifferent when it comes to details of our personal lives, we have generally refrained from inserting ourselves into the narrative by not attributing anecdotes to either one of us. It suffices to say that regardless of a story's pedigree, we both agree on the lesson drawn from it.

Can You Hear Me Now?

Henceforth, corporations will be defined less by their tangible book value and more by the "real pulsating bodies" who comprise them—stakeholders that include customers, employees, and owners. This is particularly true in an age that is heavily influenced by social media, because it organizes, amplifies, and accelerates the opportunity for those voices to be heard.

The loosely defined participatory democracy, which began in early 2011 with the Arab Spring uprisings in Egypt and elsewhere—and continued later that same year with the Twitter-induced beat downs of fee policies at Bank of America and Verizon—has clearly migrated to the workplace. Think about it: cohorts of workers (at all levels) organize on their own, show up virtually or in person at a work site, do their thing, disband, and do it all over again somewhere else.

To be sure, the terms of the deal in the workplace have morphed radically over the past decade, to a point where most managements no longer enjoy the benefit of the doubt of their workers. The terms *employer* and *job* have lost nearly all relationship to what they meant just 20 years ago. So much so that in the case of the former, British management scholar Charles Handy suggests that we should give up the term entirely and refer to ourselves not as *employers* but as *organizers of work*. Chew on that for a minute or two.

Things like worker engagement get pretty tricky when most of our workers are, as my son put it, "not married to their jobs, but just dating them"—and sometimes not even exclusively.

The Core of Our Philosophy

Before going further, let's get something straight. Our message concerning enlightened employee relations has nothing whatsoever to do with altruism. Instead, it's all about capitalism, pure and simple. Motivated people move faster, the net result being fewer problems and better business outcomes.

Charles Hampden-Turner of the London Business School puts it another way: "It's not just wrong to exploit workers, it's stupid. . . . The trouble with crushing workers is that then you have to try to make high-quality products with crushed people."

Are the concepts of "satisfied people" and capitalism mutually exclusive? Of course not! In fact, they are inextricably linked. There are those, however, who report to work each morning reciting a mantra that goes a little like this: "We're here for one reason and one reason only—to enhance shareholder wealth," and that's okay. But in our view, a problem emerges when that laudable goal is allowed to become the narrow or even exclusive focus of attention. To wit, the organization may actually be precluded from doing certain things that would otherwise best serve shareholder interests in the long run.

Levi Strauss's retired chairman, Robert Haas, apparently agrees: "Everyone looks at the wrong end of the telescope, as if profits drive the business. Financial reporting doesn't get to the real stuff—employee morale, turnover, consumer satisfaction, on-time delivery, consumer attitudes, perceptions of the brand, purchase intentions—that drives financial results."[1]

Your Reputation Is Worth More Than You Think

What is your reputation as an employer worth? What sort of things should you be doing to maintain and enhance that reputation? While we can debate what those things are, some standards must exist. Organizations that don't measure up tend to be viewed as an "employer of last resort"—places where nobody with any brains, ability, or motivation would want to work! When this occurs, only two things can happen. Either the organization is forced to pay market-premium wages and salaries in an attempt to secure better applicants, or it must accept the lower-quality applicants . . . or do both. And although the impact of bad hiring won't show up in the earnings for this quarter or next, it *will* show up.

From the start, Nevada-based Zappos has been deadly serious about operating a high-touch Internet retail business through a focused, fired-up, capably led workforce. Their people, all of whom are initially trained as telephone customer service reps, are given considerable latitude in dealing with customers. There are no scripts and no maximum call handle times. As a result, they are zealots about recruitment and training.

During an October 2011 tour of their operation, I was utterly amazed by the sincerity of their approach, the transparency of their operation (a big white board on the second floor of their office displays critical operating data replete with financial statements for everyone to see), and the esprit de corps that ensues. If Zappos and others like them have talented people practically begging to work there, do you suppose their managers find the task of recruiting easier or harder? Do they have to pay people relatively more or less to work there?

Pragmatic Ideals

If we boil all this down, what emerges is a set of beliefs and practices driven mainly by a great sense of pragmatism. According to Haas, "I believe that if you create an environment that your people identify with, that is responsive to their sense of values, justice, fairness, ethics, compassion, and appreciation, they will help you be successful. There's no guarantee, but I will stake all my chips on this vision."

Look at What Works, and Emulate It

So why not do what Zappos, Levi Strauss, and other employers of choice have done—build an organization full of capitalists, people with pride and a critical stake in the enterprise? Let's look at the situation logically. It's a simple physics problem . . . say management wants one thing, and employees want the opposite; there are more employees than managers, and the side with the most mass and energy is going to prevail. For as long as this goal incongruence exists, each side is going to spend its time accumulating or withholding energy rather than being productive. In the end, everybody loses.

Hopefully, we can all accept the premise that despite all the change in the workplace, Contented Cows STILL Give Better Milk, and that better milk (i.e., better organizational outcomes) is a good thing. Consistent with that premise, our real goal should be to have nothing but competent Contented Cows in our pasture. We must approach this objective on two fronts:

1. By hiring and retaining only those people with the capacity to be both productive and satisfied in our organization.

2. By keeping them tightly focused on our reason for existence, while rooting out and preventing distractions, which, over time, only sap their energy and enthusiasm. The trick once they are contented is to keep them that way—and therefore productive for the long haul.

Make no mistake; Contented Cow companies do both with purpose and conviction.

Robert Owen and Scottish Millworkers

The concept of Contented Cows is certainly not new. It has some impressive historical precedent both in the United States and abroad. Even in cases where the concept's application has been flawed (and there have been several), it teaches us valuable lessons.

For the first quarter of the nineteenth century, Robert Owen owned and operated a highly successful cotton mill at New Lanark in southwestern Scotland. Before visions of kilted lads and lassies frolicking in the heather fill your head, you should know that to work in a factory during Britain's industrial revolution was no day at the loch. Scotland's industrial belt at the time was home to poverty, backbreaking labor, and deplorable working conditions. But Owen believed that one's character was a product both of inherited nature and of one's environment. Knowing he could do nothing to affect the former, he conducted an experiment in the latter and created, for a time, one of Britain's most flourishing and profitable corporations—with a large labor force enjoying working conditions far surpassing the low standards of that era.

Owen inherited a population of just under 1,000 demoralized, unproductive workers whom he gradually transformed into a group of 2,500 industrious and—compared with most of their fellow countrymen—relatively satisfied members of society. He accomplished this feat simply by creating a work climate more conducive to human effort and then gradually enriching the pot.

While his competitors worked their people 13 or 14 hours a day, the beneficent Owen required only 10.5 hours a day from the adults in the mill and less than that from the children (who, when they weren't working, attended the schools he had built for them). Although even those hours seem draconian by today's standards, it was a groundbreaking development in early Victorian Britain.

Turnover was a problem for Owen's contemporaries—not so much because workers quit but because they had the annoying habit of dying, often in their 30s. Although there was not much field research on which Owen could base his hypothesis, he theorized that creating a community in which workers could live to a ripe old age and focus their energy on their work, rather than their problems, could only bring in more profits for him and his partner. His theory proved to be valid, and over more than a generation, it made him a wealthy man.

The mill town, beautifully preserved today in a popular attraction on the banks of the River Clyde near Glasgow, not only promised humane treatment of workers and more reasonable working conditions but featured a strong emphasis on education. All employees' children, from the age of two, were enrolled in superior schools in the village. Shopping, health care, and even social outlets and recreation were provided, all without leaving New Lanark.

What motivated Robert Owen to make such sweeping changes? From the outset, he seemed very much a capitalist. He figured that workers who were distracted by trying to survive couldn't possibly produce as much for him as people who at least had a fighting chance of attending to their own basic needs. Even Frederick Engels, unabashed socialist and coauthor of the infamous Communist Manifesto, said that Owen's philosophy and practices were "based upon this purely business foundation, the outcome, so to say, of commercial calculation. Throughout, [his practices] maintained this practical character."

In later years, Owen lost sight of the pragmatism that Engels recognized in him, became preoccupied with developing a utopian society, and screwed the whole thing up. Eventually, social idealism overtook the straightforward, practical ideology on which New Lanark was founded, and the community—along with the American counterpart in New Harmony, Indiana, that Owen had established—failed. Both stopped emphasizing the honor of labor, and the paternalism that evolved in its place attracted loafers and bums who liked the idea of being taken care of.[2]

Milton Hershey and the Town That Chocolate Built

A century later, another pragmatist built a community, one that remains today—a community built of chocolate.

Milton S. Hershey stumbled onto candy making after a series of small failed enterprises collapsed behind him. He literally went from rags to riches in four short years, and in the process, he built the town of Hershey, Pennsylvania. Some said his success was due to his willingness to peel off his coat and work beside any of his workers any time. Others said it was the candy maker's motto: "Stick to it" (the pun probably didn't even occur to him). Still others attributed his company's explosive and then sustained growth to Hershey's recognition that if you take care of people's certain basic needs, they can concentrate on their work and make money for you. (As evidenced by Hershey's 49.5 percent average annual return on equity over the past decade, they've done quite well in this regard.)

Hershey's practical approach to the business he built emanated not so much from ideology but from necessity. When he decided to build a chocolate factory, he couldn't afford to buy land in the more developed areas of his home state of Pennsylvania. However, the price of land in the central part of the state was very attractive. There was only one problem; nobody lived out there. Undaunted, Hershey built not just a chocolate plant but an entire town. He made housing available and built schools, a bank, a hotel (stay there if you ever have the chance), churches, parks, golf courses, and a zoo. He even installed an extensive trolley system to provide transportation for those who settled in the new town of Hershey. Rather than laying off and retrenching during the Great Depression, Hershey hired and grew.

Ruminate on This

Times have changed, and a company's practices today must reflect its operating environment. People in Victorian Scotland needed shelter, medicine, hours that wouldn't kill them, and education for their children. And crass as it may sound, Robert Owen knew that every young widowed mother mourning the premature death of her husband represented another fully consuming but unproductive member of society. His plan simply gave people more of what helped them and less of what dragged them down.

Similarly, Milton Hershey wasn't interested in offering his chocolatiers a sweet deal at his expense. In his time and place, the only affordable option meant going to the frontier. People are doing the very same thing today; it's just that they often find that frontier in places like India and China. Hershey's plan would work only if he could provide productive workers with a town, or at least a way to get to the factory. Otherwise, who would make the chocolate?

It's not about social protectionism or paternalism—anything but. When people are afforded the opportunity to focus freely on their work—an opportunity backed by high expectations and appropriate rewards— they'll do their jobs. It's really a very wise thing for an organization to create and support a satisfied workforce, because that workforce can build wealth almost as fast as a disgruntled one can destroy it.

As we continue to make the case about Contented Cows with cold, hard facts and analyze what it takes to create and maintain a capably led, satisfied, highly motivated workforce, you can expect us to poke some holes in the myths that abound about what employee satisfaction really is. We're willing to bet it's probably not what you think.

Chapter Summary

1. Productivity comes from people, not machines.
2. The notion of Contented Cows is anything but new. We've known for a long time that people can choose to contribute if (but only if) they want to.
3. People factors are a source of competitive advantage or disadvantage; the choice is yours.
4. Contented Cow companies have absolutely, positively outgrown, outearned, and outperformed their competitors and the broader market over a 25-year period.
5. The argument is for capitalism, not cynicism or humanism.

Cows with Attitude

You can make a happy person into a good worker, but not necessarily the other way around.

—Gordon Segal, founder, Crate & Barrel

Where Does Contentment Begin?

We have a healthy suspicion that some of you might be muttering things under your breath like, "Let's dispense with all this idealistic 'happy-go-lucky' stuff. My employees are what they are. Some of them enjoy working here and give every appearance of being energized by their work, and others don't. They're just *not* contentable, and I don't see that changing!" You could well be right.

Let's clarify something. The job of "morale maintenance" in your organization doesn't rest entirely on your—or management's—shoulders. In fact, we agree wholeheartedly with noted organizational change consultant Price Pritchett, who admonishes us in his book, *New Habits for a Radically Changing World*, that we must "manage our own morale." Nobody should have to handhold their workforce until they "feel good about things." Indeed, each of us is responsible for our own happiness. But we think you'll produce better results in a classic struggle between principle and pragmatism if—as an influencer of organizational culture and practices—you take reasonable steps that are well within your grasp to promote workplace satisfaction. And you should do it because it's in your own best interest.

As noted in Jeb Blount's wonderful book, *People Follow You*, "Leadership can be loosely defined as a process of organizing, inspiring, focusing, and enabling others to follow you in the interest of getting something done. Heretofore, the operative words in that definition might have been solely the ones ending in -ing. But that was then. More so today, the 'you' is of increasing importance, not because leadership is *about* you (it's not) but . . . because people have lost faith in so many of the institutions around them [including] their employers. As they disengage from the institution, they choose instead to align with and follow individual leaders, at work, in churches, and in their communities. In short, people follow you. And you means YOU." Ergo, it is very much worth it to you, as a leader, to want to earn that benefit of the doubt, and the discretionary effort that goes along with it. And no, you don't earn it by going soft on people.

At any given time, most managers have at least three challenges with respect to worker motivation and satisfaction, *all* of which involve basic questions about human psychology and its relationship to morale:

1. Hiring people who have the potential to be both productive and satisfied in your particular environment.

2. Turning things around if the majority of the people at work are, shall we say, less than ecstatic already (mad cows, perhaps?). One way or another, you do have to play the hand you were dealt.

3. Keeping them on track once you get them there.

At its very core, the whole notion of people being a distinct source of competitive advantage hinges on the way organizations and individual leaders perceive their workforces and the nature of the employment relationship. Do you see people on the asset or the liability side of the balance sheet? Are employees an opportunity—that is, a source of strategic advantage—or a cost to be reckoned with and minimized whenever possible? Are they viewed as little more than plug-and-play cogs in the operating process? Or do you see them as real, pulsating, thinking, idea-generating, responsibility-taking assets?

Sadly, virtually all of the economic models, attendant planning processes, and business metrics see something other than "human capital." Instead, they seem to be front-loaded with the assumption that people don't like to work, don't want to work, and won't work without exceptional and costly external stimuli. And it's that same behavior modeling theory that still insists a "supervisor" is needed for every seven or eight worker bees.

Last year, I keynoted a conference for a large association of companies that rely on home-based workers for all of their production output. Since we don't kiss and tell, let's just call them Acme Supply Company and refer to their employees as "operators" (people who are, by the way, classified as employees and not contractors). As is our custom, I conducted phone interviews with a few future audience members to gain some added context relative to their business prior to the event.

One of the interviewees was the co-owner and president of a firm that employs 230 of these "operators." He informed me that these 230 people, mostly women, all worked from home and were geographically dispersed across the southeastern United States. When I asked him how many he had met personally, he quickly responded, "None of them" and then elaborated by saying, "Truth be known, I don't even know the names of more than a handful." While still on the phone with this gentleman, I flashed back to the animal research referenced in Chapter 1 that suggests that dairy cows produce upward of 60 extra gallons of milk per year when called by name. I had to swallow hard to choke down the question I really wanted to ask him: "How hard do you think these people are working for you right now?"

Peach Limbs Don't Grow on Oaks

A major assumption operating in most businesses is that they exist to make a profit. (At least we know it is in ours.) Hence, nearly all of our behavior responds to that assumption. If we're going to discuss the kinds of practices that will transform your business into a grass-bellied, milk-producing Contented Cow, we first have to deal with the beliefs on which your company operates. All of the smart, innovative practices in the world will fall flat if they're inconsistent with the prevailing assumptions.

To be sustainable over time, your practices must line up with your assumptions. Diversity management pioneer Roosevelt Thomas said it quite succinctly: "Peach limbs don't grow on oaks."[1] He was referring to the fact that a peach limb grafted onto an oak tree will actually appear to live for a brief time, only to soon fall off dead. Similarly, you can fake practices you don't believe in for a while, but you won't be able to pull it off over the long haul.

Although Dr. Thomas originally made the comparison in another context, his metaphor describes precisely what happens in any field where the principles of organizational behavior theory apply. If you start changing your workplace practices without examining the assumptions that drive them, you'll likely be disappointed. And you'll likely make arbitrary, weakly executed, short-lived, and, to be sure, costly changes.

On the other hand, if you examine your assumptions about your employees, their human nature, which side of the balance sheet they're on, what they need to succeed, and how much (or how little) it will take to provide that and find yourself deficient, you may end up modifying some of your assumptions a little. New practices can emerge from these adjustments, practices that are more consistent with your frame of mind and thus more likely to succeed. In short, if you'll only stop kidding yourself, your chances for experiencing real change will increase exponentially.

> *Fortunately, even when cows are left up to their own devices, they seldom develop poor temperament and vices.*
> —"Improving the Welfare of Dairy Cows Through Management"[2]

You Get What You Expect to Get

So what do you assume about the people who work in your organization? What do you assume about people in general?

If you travel this mortal coil believing that most people who would come to work for you are lazy, stupid, untrustworthy, or mean-spirited, that assumption can't help but show up in the way you run your business. You'll invent all kinds of rules and procedures designed for numbskulls who couldn't pour milk out of a boot with the directions printed on the heel. You'll no doubt have a warden—er, supervisor—for every six or seven folks and will inevitably attract just the kind of people who match your assumptions. Discerning, competent employees won't come anywhere near your place, thereby reinforcing your original assumption.

There is a reason that the crowds drawn to parades consistently outnumber those that attend funerals. Most people are far more attracted by hope, optimism, and freedom than by negativism and restriction. I want to work with and for people who believe that together we can do great things that *matter*.

People will not follow a pessimistic leader for long, nor will they perform particularly well for that person. If you truly expect to get the benefit of a person or team's best effort, each person needs to sense that you have faith that he or she can and will deliver. Otherwise, all bets are off.

Several years ago, a professional football team was about a third of the way into a pretty dismal season. The team's coach was quoted in the local media as saying that his team was so awful that he didn't expect them to win another game all season. Guess what? They didn't. Not because the coach was clairvoyant, but because they were merely living down to his expectations.

This example is indicative of the wider problem at all levels of business: you are likely to get just the kind of behavior from employees that you expect. And, paradoxically, they will either live up or down to your expectations because your policies, procedures, and employment practices had at their bedrock those same assumptions.

Core Covenants

Organizations operate on a limited number, not a great long list, of core beliefs and assumptions that are "burned in" to the very fabric of the business. Here are a few you should adopt and begin operating on today.

1. *The Rule of Common Purpose:* You should run the organization in a way that permits all legitimate stakeholders—managers, employees, owners, and customers—to benefit, each in their own way. In other words, we must take care to ensure that the interests of each core constituent are meaningfully represented. Of course, this doesn't make everyone an equal equity partner. But we need to recognize

that, regardless of the endeavor, each of us is silently (usually) asking the question, "What's in it for me?" (Or "WIIFM?") Until you satisfactorily address that question, you really can't unleash much productive effort.

2. *The Rule of Selective Membership:* Since the beginning of time, winning organizations the world over have recognized and held dear the notion that membership is a privilege (a rare one, in fact), and not a right. The U.S. Marines boast about it externally in their branding ("The Few, The Proud, The Marines") and internally as a way of maintaining esprit de corps. American Express has anchored its brand on the notion that their "members" or cardholders earn more—and thus spend more. Each is intended as a sign of selectivity, denoting membership among an elite cadre of people.

   The foundation of every smart recruiting process is the axiom that "our organization may be a great place to work, but it's not for everybody. In fact, it's not even for most people." Contrary to popular belief, there really is an ample supply of talented, hardworking, honest people available—some of whom already work for you. Your job, your most important job in fact, is to find others like them. Of course, you've got to expend a little effort doing it, and find them one at a time, because eagles don't flock, but they are out there. Get started today!

   Those who have heard us speak or have read our second book, *Contented Cows MOOve Faster,* have heard us mention in glowing terms the Pebble Beach Company (PBC), a wonderful northern California resort. A few years ago, in an effort to get closer to a client, I worked as a greeter at the Pebble Beach Pro Shop during the annual AT&T Pebble Beach National Pro-Am Golf Tournament. For me, it was a great way to find out what it was really like working for our client up close and in person.

   One morning at 0-dark 30, I rode the crew bus from an off-site parking lot to my duty post at the pro shop. As the only passenger on the bus, I chatted up the driver and asked her if she liked working at PBC. She said she did and that she liked in particular the fact that "not just anybody can get a job here." Translation: the place is pretty selective, and as a result, I don't have to work with turkeys—which also means that their guests don't have to encounter them. Cha-ching!

3. *The Rule of Omission:* Your employees, customers, and, yes, owners will usually be less inspired by what you do *for* them than by what you *don't* do *to* them. If, for example, you expect them to believe in you and stick with you, never, ever, *ever* deceive or take advantage of them! If the company conducts its business in a satisfactory way to the people who work there (you don't have to be Mr. Wonderful), most employees will produce more and better stuff. Consistent with this admonition is the following short list of actions that are virtually guaranteed to bring someone's best effort to a screeching halt:

   a. Do not under any circumstances lie to them.

   b. Don't take them for granted.

   c. Do not keep them in the dark.

   d. Don't ever humiliate them.

At one stage in my career, my boss's boss was a rather devious and mean-spirited sort who had gotten his job for reasons that had nothing to do with merit. By and large, he ruled through intimidation. One day, I got a call from this fellow while out of town on business. I could tell from the slightly "tinny" quality of the audio that he was on a speakerphone. He spent about 10 minutes tearing me limb from limb over something I've now completely forgotten about. What I have not forgotten, though, is that shortly after we hung up, I got a call from one of my peers to alert me that she had been in this bozo's office during the call—along with two of my direct reports, another of my peers, and a vendor. From that moment on, he never got my best effort, and to this day I'm fairly certain that if I saw that guy in a crosswalk, my vehicle would suffer unfortunate momentary brake failure.

Bogus Assumptions

Unfortunately, we have seen too many organizations operating on one or more of the following very erroneous and dangerous assumptions:

- People need paternalistic employers who will take care of them, because they are incapable of taking care of themselves.

- The more we give people without expecting anything in return, the happier and better off they'll be.
- Running a "kinder, gentler" organization will foster love, siblinghood, peace, and goodwill.

Indeed, the bankruptcies of two of the largest American automobile manufacturers and several commercial airlines bear witness to the folly of these premises.

Assumptions Are a Two-Way Street: The Employees' Perspective

Assumptions would be immensely simpler to handle if you had to mind only your own. The problem is everyone else has a set as well. Of equal importance to your assumptions about your workforce is the whole question of *theirs*—about work, the organization, and you personally.

For example, what do they assume about profit? How much is there? Where does it come from? Where does it go? A good part of the impetus behind the 2011 Occupy Wall Street (and various other cities) demonstrations centered on these questions. Protestors (both present and at home) who believed that they had been pushed into a corner by two-plus years of vicious recession and a fairly jobless recovery took the position that none of the profits seemed to be finding their way to them—thus, something sinister must be in play. And the 99 percent versus 1 percent debate was born.

Something similar is involved in the continuing erosion of the trust factor in the workplace. What are employees' assumptions when they show up for work in the morning? Are they fully engaged? Or is it more like, "I know they're out to screw me, so I'll get them first?" Would you even know? How?

What do they assume are the organization's current priorities? Have they had to figure this one out on their own, or have you told them? Clearly? Are you sure?

And what are their assumptions about *you*? What do they think is important to you? What you stand for? Believe in? What will or won't you tolerate? Yes, we know; you probably told everyone this stuff when you hired them, right? But how long ago was that, and have your actions really been consistent with those statements made so long ago? In other words, what's your authenticity level?

Unless you and your entire management team have invested considerable personal time and effort communicating honestly and openly—sharing the bad news as well as the good, showing people the numbers, helping them understand them, and making sure that your actions back up your words—we would bet that you've got people operating with bad data. In other words, your organization very well could be afflicted with a bad case of ignorance . . . curable, but ignorance nonetheless. And as author and SRC Holdings founder and chief executive officer (CEO) Jack Stack pointed out in his book *The Great Game of Business*, "Ignorance Can Kill a Company!"[3]

What Employees Want: The Contented Cows' View

Leaders of Contented Cow companies understand that although their people have individual preferences, there is a common list of things they want (and deserve)—things that are necessary to fully engaging with the enterprise:

1. *Meaningful Work:* People want and need to be proud of their work. They want suitable challenges and the freedom to pursue them. They want to be in the game, not on the bench.

2. *High Standards:* They don't want to associate with losers. We all tend to moan and whine about high standards, but deep down, every one of us realizes that these standards are a necessary component to winning.

3. *A Clear Sense of Purpose and Direction:* People want to read mysteries, not live them. Timely, relevant, and meaningful (i.e., truthful) information is a must. Where are we going, and why? Why does it matter? How does my role fit in?

4. *Balanced "Worth-its":* Managers must demonstrate a commensurate level of interest and investment in employees. We must provide internal systems that support rather than impede their efforts and give them the freedom to pursue some things that are important to them. Two of the most powerful motivators in today's workplace

are (a) having the opportunity to learn and build skills (and your résumé) and (b) being able to do your very best work. We want to see some progress made at the end of each day, and it drives us crazy when silly, systemic obstacles keep us from doing our best.

5. *A Level Playing Field:* Employees want reciprocal caring, coupled with some sense of justice and an assurance they won't be taken advantage of.

6. *To Be and Feel Competent:* We don't really need to explain this one, do we?

The "Happy Curve"

Most of this book deals with what happens to people at work—the way they're treated, informed (or not), and related to. But it's only fair to devote a little attention to a discussion about "contentability"—the capacity to be contented. None of the other ideas and examples we introduce will do you any good if you have a whole field full of irascible beasts.

In an article that appeared in *Business Horizons* magazine, writer Dennis Organ advanced the theory that workplace morale depends not only on the work environment but to some degree on the internal sense of happiness that employees possess or lack. In other words, hiring inherently happy people can exponentially boost the morale of the organization as a whole.[4]

We think it's a given that in order to have contented employees, you have to start with "contentable" ones. We all know people who seem to be happy no matter what, as well as those who aren't happy with anything. Some people are always looking for a scapegoat, and the workplace is a target-rich environment. So does job satisfaction depend on what happens to us at work? How we are treated? The so-called working conditions? Or is it an individual's emotional makeup? We tend to agree with Robert Owen, implementer of pragmatic reforms at his Scottish cotton mill, who believed that it was likely a product of both.

Organ's story of Jack Davis makes an interesting case. Davis, a former corporate executive, unscientifically formulated the idea of what he called the Happy Curve when he had the opportunity to take over a company in crisis. His new environment was a nightmare for shareholders and a really bad place to work; almost everyone was miserable, and with good reason. But there was a small but solid core of upbeat, supportive, and optimistic people. Careful, deliberate observation of these people caused Davis and his staff (none of whom were trained psychologists) to conclude that these folks were just plain cheerful people, on or off the job. They had stable and fulfilling family lives, interests outside of work, and confidence in their abilities. Ups and downs were part of their lives too, but on balance they were comfortable in their own skin and stayed on a pretty even and relatively elevated keel.

Now consider the possibility, as Davis did, that each individual has a range of moods. High for one person may be average for another, and some people would never get as low as others. In fact, each person might have a sort of emotional set point (like the one that's supposed to be anchoring our weight) toward which moods tend to gravitate, unless something really unusual is going on.

Moreover, Davis and his crew came to believe that they had somehow ended up with a disproportionately high number of people with low Happy Curves. In other words, the grouches had reached critical mass. Since morale is a group dynamic more than an individual condition, the abundance of low Happy Curves alone was enough to drag down the others at least a little.

As the business grew and attrition created openings, Davis made a conscious effort to hire people who not only were qualified but seemed to have the potential for being happy. Although no one was ever fired for being sullen (perhaps they should have been), the organization eventually took on a new, more positive outlook. Sales improved, and the spiral turned upward. Of course, higher morale was not the single silver bullet that saved this company, but it was obviously an integral factor.

A "Sticky" Variable

As it turns out, a number of research studies corroborate Davis's experience. What we call "morale" is, according to University of California, Berkeley professor Barry Staw, described as a "sticky" variable. That means some of it is accounted for by what is innate, as opposed to being caused by environmental factors. For example, when organizational psychologists measure the job satisfaction of a group of people at two points in time separated by intervals of up to several years, the best and most consistent predictor of job satisfaction at the later time is the *earlier* assessment of job satisfaction. This finding holds up even when many people in the group have changed jobs or employers.

A study of 5,000 adults begun by the National Institute on Aging in 1973 found that the happiest of people in that year were still relatively happy 10 years later, regardless of changes in their work or other circumstances.[5] Perhaps most telling, Staw and his research associates found that a high school counselor's rating of the "cheerfulness" of adolescents predicted their job satisfaction 30 years later as well—or better than any single aspect of their jobs! Also persuasive are the results of studies of identical twins separated at birth, indicating that 30 percent or more of the variation in adult job satisfaction relates to genetic factors.[6] There might be something to this sticky variable business, but, of course, it's not the whole story.

We're not suggesting that work environment doesn't matter. You've had good jobs and bad ones, and you know there's a difference. But we do think there's good reason to believe that people vary in their tendencies to experience good morale—within a range—regardless of environmental factors. Retired Marriott CEO Bill Marriott apparently feels the same way, which is why he implored managers to hire those who have the manners and "spirit to serve," preferring to train people in other skills they might need. Unfortunately, you can't teach nice. Any company would do well to adopt a similar philosophy when recruiting.

You can, by the way, hire "for fit" and still uphold your organization's commitment to equal employment opportunity. There aren't any gender, racial, or ethnic differences in the tendency to be happy. (Indeed, the only acceptable discrimination in hiring practices should be directed against grouches!)

But Will They Be Contented Here?

We have made the case from the start that Contented Cow companies are great places to work. And although this is an absolute fact, it's also a fact that all cows aren't going to be content living on your ranch. Contented

Cow companies unabashedly take steps to ensure that people who won't fit in with their particular environment don't go to work there (and that they don't last long if they do somehow manage to get on the payroll). In effect, what they recognize—and it's as true in your company as it is in theirs—is that not everyone would be happy, productive, or successful working there.

For some, the selection process actually extends past the new hire's start date. Zappos is so committed to getting the fit right with each hire that they offer new employees $2,000 to leave during their new hire training if for any reason they feel the fit isn't a good one.

Such measures not only narrow the risk but also make plain from the start just how serious the organization is about employment matters. Moreover, their meticulous care has the beneficial side effect of confirming for the individual that he or she is joining an elite organization, thus creating high expectations, which, in turn, breed high performance. During a tour of the Zappos operation, our tour guide volunteered that despite what one might expect, very few people take the money and leave.

One measure of a person's capacity to be satisfied and productive at your company is the degree to which that person can live with your ground rules. Every organization has certain things that they consider sacrosanct and immutable. Changing them just isn't up for discussion. Among other things, Contented Cow companies realize the absolute futility of trying to convert someone whose internal compass points 40 degrees to the left or right of the corporation's.

It's not a matter of morality but of makeup. More so than the average company, Contented Cow companies have a crystal clear sense of direction and a keen awareness of their core values. Accordingly, they tend to take very strong positions on anything that impinges on those values and have little room for those who are unwilling to make the journey with them or are otherwise unsuited to their demanding standards.

> *Many herds allow their cows to develop their own individual personalities as long as it does not mean special care and treatment . . . Individual cows must fit into the system rather than the system conforming to the habits of the cow.*
> —"Improving the Welfare of Dairy Cows Through Management"[7]

Chick-fil-A: Never On Sunday

You can't get a Chick-fil-A chicken sandwich—or anything else on the quick-service chain's menu—on a Sunday, because each and every one of their stores is closed that day. If you want to know why, read founder Truett Cathy's book, *It's Easier to Succeed Than to Fail*. In reality, it doesn't matter why. That's just the way they've chosen to run their business. Although they could probably increase sales by opening their stores on Sunday, they're happy to leave that to McDonald's and others. Before you assume that they are too old-fashioned for their own good, consider the fact that the majority of Cathy's stores do more business in six days than their competitors do in seven.

In an age when body art of all types, extreme hairstyles, and freedom of individual expression are evident everywhere, some organizations remain resolute in their insistence on conservative personal appearance standards. FedEx, Marriott, and Disney, for example, are fanatical about their people's appearance and anything else that the customer/guest comes into contact with. Although Disney reversed a long-standing no-beard policy for theme park employees in early 2012, you can be quite certain that the only thing that stands out in their parks is the costumed characters, and that's the way they want it.

As speed of execution becomes an ever-greater factor in our lives, companies are increasingly emphasizing a person's ability to learn and quickly master new information and concepts. The learning curve for most jobs is steeper and shorter, and forgiveness for newbies is practically nonexistent. Hence, if you can't demonstrate the ability to quickly grasp new information, you're toast.

According to Fox Sports analyst and former football coach Jimmy Johnson, a player has to be teachable. An unteachable player will be miserable personally and fail the team at crucial moments. Johnson amplified the point in his book, *Turning the Thing Around*, when he said, "We evaluate a helluva lot more than vertical leap and forty-yard dash times. If I'm talking with a group of prospective draftees and one kid's sitting there flipping ice at his teammate, he'll be hard pressed to sit on my list for more than about five minutes. I have formal training in the psychology of learning, but none of that does any good on an unwilling or uncaring pupil."[8]

> *Get good people and expect them to perform. Terminate them quickly and fairly if you make the wrong choice.*
>
> —J. Willard Marriott Jr.[9]

Time after time, in organization after organization, the winners are absolute zealots about who will and won't get to play on their team. According to former A.G. Edwards CEO Ben Edwards, "We want someone with character who shares our values and who will fit into our culture. We're looking for a long term happy marriage."[10] More often than not, they rely on the intangible factors rather than raw credentials or ability when making that decision.

The fast-growing and financially successful Chick-fil-A chain has a uniquely positive corporate culture. Operational expertise alone is not enough to cut it there. Truett Cathy says he looks at a person's character as much as anything else when he hires an employee or contracts with an operator for one of his growing number of stores.

Chick-fil-A's selectivity pays off in more ways than one. Their employee turnover rates, for example, consistently run at a fraction of the industry average. Other companies should take a cue from the chain and reorient their recruitment and selection processes by hiring "for fit" rather than mere credentials.

Contentability and Corporate Assimilation

We know that we've just advised you to hire only those people who will be able to fit in or assimilate to your culture. And we suspect some readers may have a problem with organizations that, at least in their eyes, impose undue requirements for assimilation. Such prerequisites can be a double-edged sword. Organizations that require people to fit in by meeting arbitrary or irrelevant considerations often filter out potential top performers who don't fit the irrelevant part of their mold. For example, a company that insists that a woman behave like "one of the guys" or that people leave integral aspects of their identity at the door puts the wrong filter on the selection process.

The other edge of this sword is that strong leaders of outstanding organizations realize that many very talented people will not be able to meet the requirements necessary to succeed in their Contented Cow companies. These people won't be happy, productive, or successful working there—no matter what. What sets these companies apart, though, is that they actually do something about the realization. Their assimilation criteria are strictly business-oriented, deliberate, and rational and do not consist of conveniences, preferences, or unquestioned traditions.

Every organization requires some degree of assimilation. You must be completely in touch with the real requirements for success in your business and highly disciplined in proclaiming those things loudly, clearly, and unashamedly to all who would invest their time and hopes in working there. Ultimately, as Roosevelt Thomas puts it, "People will always have to salute certain organizational flags. The job of the leader is to be very clear about which flags need to be saluted."

Company standards and assimilation criteria exist for a reason—one that frequently has to do with the customer. For example, FedEx has gotten the message loud and clear from literally hundreds of customer focus group sessions that they prefer a neatly attired, clean-cut look—that is, no beards. The way the company sees it, as much money as you're paying to do business with them, they're only too happy to oblige.

Disney is every bit as emphatic about the use of coarse language. In fact, we're quite certain their "cast members" would be fired for using some of the words in this book. But if you fathom the simple logic behind Disney's requirement, it has a lot to do with the fact that the majority of what they sell is based on an image of clean, wholesome entertainment for some very impressionable kids.

It's no less the case at Marriott, where only about 10 percent of job applicants pass muster. If an applicant is at all uncomfortable with their clean-living, extremely service-conscious environment, he or she will not make it there. Some would say that the Marriott way has its roots in the company's Mormon-influenced origins, and they might be right. But as frequent Marriott guests, we can tell you that it most assuredly makes a difference—wherever it comes from. As proof that we put our money where our mouths are, large chunks of this book were written while holed up in various Marriott hotels around the country.

The Proof Is in the People

Although the Contented Cow companies are unique in many ways, they share remarkable commonality in three important respects. The rest of this book is going to hang on these three branches (no speed-reading).

Day in and day out, each of them does a remarkable job of:

1. Getting (and keeping) their people solidly lined up behind the organization's core purpose and objectives. In short, they're *Committed* (capital "C" intentional).

2. Letting people know through a myriad of ways, some large (but mostly small), that they're important. They're more than just a number or body; they are *Cared about*.

3. Through personal as well as systemic means, removing the obstacles from the path of their workforce. In short, they *Enable* their people to do their very best work.

Contented Cows Are:
- Committed
- Cared about
- Enabled

In the following chapters, we'll address each of these areas by addressing the following questions:

1. What exactly are the *components* of a given characteristic? How will you recognize it when you see it?

2. How can you *replicate* it? There are two aspects of this equation:

   a. *Employee engagement practices:* These are things you actually do to promote contentment and productivity: compensation, information sharing, employee involvement, hiring and decision-making processes—all of this and more.

b. *Operational practices:* All the decisions you make about running the business that aren't directed at employee relations, but which employees nonetheless must depend on or contend with. These are less obvious, because they won't come up in a discussion of employee relations. However, they have a tremendous effect on both contentedness and frustration levels. They include things such as customer service policies, safety, and equipment maintenance.

3. What are the *employees' responsibilities* in all of this? What must people do to ensure their own contentment? This is anything but a one-way street.

4. Finally, to help you three-dimensionalize the ideas governing each chapter, we'll identify some of the people and organizations that are doing an especially good job in these areas. From time to time, we'll also take a look at those that have "climbed the mountain" but, due to a failed strategy in other respects, have lost ground or ceased to exist altogether.

Our job, then, will be to pick through the situations and examples, bringing to light those that define each characteristic in the simplest, clearest, and most replicable manner.

Chapter Summary

1. No less than they affect virtually every other outcome in our lives, our assumptions about people drive our leadership practices—and, in turn, the outcome of our relationship with them. In other words, you get what you expect. Practices that are inconsistent with your organization's operating assumptions are doomed to fail.

2. Never lose sight, even for a moment, of the expectations of employees in a Contented Cow company, most notably:

   o Meaningful work

   o High standards

- o Clear purpose and direction
- o Balanced "Worth-its"
- o A level playing field
- o Ability to be and feel competent

3. Similarly, don't allow yourself to become distracted by the bogus assumptions that are often put before us, particularly those advocating kinder and gentler standards (or no standards at all), blatant paternalism, or the need to give or pay more without good and compelling reason.

4. Hire for fit and not just talent. Make sure the "fit" requirements are relevant to business success, but then stick with them, no matter what.

5. Remember that not everyone's going to be content living on your ranch.

6. Contented Cows are:
- o Committed
- o Cared about
- o Enabled

Contented Cows
Are Committed

The "Vision Thing": Passengers or Crew

It doesn't take a genius to figure out that in an environment where there is a shared vision of excellence . . . where people can be the best they can be on a daily basis . . . where, when they know what is expected of them . . . understand that reward is linked to performance . . . and BELIEVE they can make a difference because they will be heard . . . they WILL make a difference. They will go BEYOND our expectations and great things will start to happen.
—FedEx founder, chairman, and CEO Frederick W. Smith[1]

Every major achievement in the history of humankind has been accompanied by one thing—significant, as in capital "C," Commitment on the part of one or more people. Think about it: without real Commitment, Christopher Columbus would have waited for better maps before sailing off the edge of the known universe. Martin Luther King Jr. would not have marched in Selma, Alabama, and early NASA astronauts would have voted to send more monkeys up before strapping their butts to a relatively untested rocket.

Commitment starts with an extremely well-grasped destination or journey—a place, a concept, an overarching purpose. It answers questions such as: What are we here for? What's our raison d'être? Where are we going?

Dr. King was attempting to take a people and a nation—indeed, the entire world—to a new and different place, where the color of one's skin was no longer a boundary. Why does *your* organization exist? Where is it going? And how well do you tell that story? Who will even remember it six months from now?

Despite the billions spent every year on internal corporate communications, most companies do miserable jobs of helping their people understand the business's direction, goals, and priorities—let alone securing their Commitment. If you doubt the magnitude of this "failure to communicate" claim, take five minutes and go do some field research of your own.

Ask a sample of your employees to jot down what they believe to be the organization's three highest priorities and where they think it is headed. Do it right now, before you read another word. When the answers come back without any degree of consistency, the question is obvious: If they don't know where you're going, how can they possibly help you get there?

Don't feel too bad. We have asked this question not just of ground-level workers, but hundreds of C-level execs in our Bottom Line Leadership program, and the result is exactly the same every time: *nobody* knows. And when the top 10 or 12 people in an organization can't consistently articulate the direction or top priorities, things are really slowing down.

A leader has got to show his troops the route of the march and the destination.

—Frank Pacetta, Xerox Sales Manager[2]

Burning Off the Fog

Some organizations have people who *do* seem to "get it." We wanted to know what makes the difference between these places and the average organization. If your people know (really know) what you're all about, how did they find out? What did you, as a manager, have to do to help them realize it?

We have asked these questions of hundreds of business leaders over the past 15 years, and the answers (where there *were* cogent answers) are about as unsexy and unimaginative as it gets. We had hoped perhaps to hear of some ingenious, idiot-proof techniques guaranteed to inject the milk of human understanding into every living thing under the corporate roof, but there weren't any. Instead, we heard repeatedly from organizations whose people do seem to get it—and get it good—that you simply tell them, over, and over, and over again. In fact, you practically carpet bomb them from day one with the same simple, clear-cut, credible message. Then, you back that message up with deeds.

However, what *did* surface from these conversations were some very definable conditions that impede companies from getting people to see and support the big picture—such as:

1. *The Event Syndrome:* In all too many cases, any attempt to communicate these priorities, goals, and so on, takes place only once a year, or maybe every three or four years, usually after some mountaintop retreat or strategic planning session. Someone—or some group—produces a wonderfully crafted letter, speech, pamphlet, or video. Everyone endures the obligatory "viewing" and then promptly goes back to what they were doing, safely assured that the topic won't come up again for at least another year.

   In one organization we know, the senior management group returned from its three-day mountaintop experience in Moses-like fashion, bearing (get this) *real stone tablets* with the newly minted corporate goals inscribed on them. With phrases such as "competitively superior, highly integrated, broad-based networks" inscribed upon them, we're fairly certain that more than a few of their people couldn't even pronounce some of this stuff, let alone understand or remember it. Fortunately, those rocks made pretty good paperweights.

2. *Message of the Week:* In other cases, companies somehow expect all those thoughtful, intelligent people they call employees to buy the notion that this week they're a "Market Leader," knowing all the while that next week they'll be the "Most Operationally Efficient," "Lowest Cost Producer," or some other arbitrarily chosen superlative. Come on; get real! It's almost as if many executives are suffering from the very same attention deficit disorder that grips a lot of

our school-age children. (Maybe there should be a Ritalin prescription for the boardroom.)

3. *"Misaligned Bellybuttons" or "Talk Is Cheap"*: Basketball players learn early in their careers that the best way to anticipate movement when guarding an opponent is to watch the other person's midsection, as it reliably predicts where the rest of the person is going. The same is true off the court as well—and in some companies we find that executives' bellybuttons are pointed in one direction and their mouths in another.

4. *"Mission Statement" vs. Sense of Mission*: Comparatively speaking, executives spend entirely too much precious time and energy crafting precisely worded mission, vision, and value statements. This is time and effort they should be investing in making darned sure every human being on their payroll truly understands and appreciates what all that stuff means.

In case after case, Contented Cow companies are the ones doing the better job of helping their people see, feel, and appreciate where the business is headed, why it is going there, and what role they are expected to play. Although their efforts aren't usually the slickest or fanciest (no stone tablets, to be sure), they are clear, consistent, and "udderly" compelling.

Making It Stick

Some of the better examples we have seen involve health care companies such as Medtronic and Genentech, who routinely use patient-staff interactions as a very impactful way of reminding their people why they have a job. Indeed, buildings on Genentech's South San Francisco campus are adorned with huge murals containing pictures of patients, emphasizing the reason those buildings exist.

Another company that manufactures intravenous bags and tubing occasionally takes workers to a neighboring county hospital to witness the very real impact of their labor firsthand. Others make effective use of corporate legend, stories, and recognition programs to shape and reinforce the big picture for their staffs.

Witness Toronto's Maple Leaf Sports and Entertainment (MLSE), a company that caught our attention because of their efforts to keep their articulated mission and values alive and functioning well in everything their workers do on the job.

MLSE is in the business of producing fun, something that is in short supply in a world where people are wound way too tight. Even the company name sounds fun—and by all accounts, working there is just that. The diversified company owns four Toronto professional sports teams—the Maple Leafs (NHL) and Marlies (AHL) hockey teams, the Raptors (NBA) basketball team, and the Football Club (FC) soccer team. They also own and operate the magnificent multiuse Air Canada Centre, home of the Maple Leafs and Raptors and Canada's premiere entertainment venue, hosting dozens of live concerts and other events every year.

In addition to the usual corporate infrastructure positions, the team of more than 3,500 full- and part-time employees performs all kinds of jobs, including stage and house management, engineering, housekeeping, and work associated with quick-service restaurants, informal and fine dining, and sports broadcasting. One large, multidisciplinary team converts the venue from a hockey rink to a basketball court and then to a live concert arena, sometimes all in one day. Another runs a large retail operation vending all sorts of team gear and other enthusiast needs.

"We work hard, and a lot of people put in long and odd hours, but we're having such a good time, that nobody seems to notice," said Tanya Avoledo-Vadori, whose title with MLSE is Manager, People. "People are always saying, 'I can't believe I get to work here!'"

The company uses sports-themed vernacular to describe almost everything they do. They have an Employee Playbook and refer to new hires as Rookies. One outstanding manager, regardless of department or rank, receives the Coach of the Year award annually. And every month, the company chooses four Stars based on outstanding work that exemplifies (and reinforces) the company's four stated values:

- Excite every fan.
- Inspire our people.
- Be dedicated to our teams.
- Be leaders in our community.

In addition to the four Stars, a Player of the Month (POM) is also designated. Not only is the name of the award a twist on what so many call Employee of the Month (yawn), but the selection criteria are also different from many EOM programs we've all seen—those in which a good employee who hasn't yet had the honor gets the nod, and the attendant parking spot, for that month.

In contrast, MLSE's POM is the employee whose work is deemed to have had the most significant impact on the company's success during that month. The March 2011 recipient, Jim Steele, was recognized for his extraordinary work contributing to the Air Canada Centre's successful hosting of the live national broadcast of the Junos, Canada's Music Awards. An excerpt about his nomination reveals something of the heft of the monthly designation, as well as this recipient's qualifications for receiving it:

> After a year of advance work, the Junos loaded in, and in the span of a week, the largest stage ever built in [the Air Canada Centre] grew out of the ground. The set moved from concept to reality. The visuals were programmed, the sound and the lighting perfected. With a lot of patience, pre-planning, and some exceptionally organized chaos, our Player of the Month was able to steer the event into the success it ultimately became. Each pre, post and concurrent event was assigned and delegated. Each detail was addressed and noted. Each concern was met with options and professionalism.
>
> As the jewel event for the Canadian music industry, and a LIVE broadcast, it goes without saying that there was no room for error. The expertise of our POM brought ACC & MLSE into the nation's focus, and it was flawless. The event requirements that he oversees would make an ordinary person's head spin on the simplest of set-ups, but he conquered the most complex with ease. Most notably, he did this while defending the reputation, safety, security, code compliance and revenue potential of MLSE.

At year's end, the organization creates a roster of All Stars populated by 8 of the year's 48 value-specific Stars, two from each value. Then the entire employee population elects the year's Most Valuable Player from the 12 Players of the Month.

The seriousness with which MLSE takes these designations, and the clear linkage they make to their four values, contributes in large part to the fact that these values are baked into every job at MLSE. In fact, most MLSE employees could tell you without having to refer to the Employee Playbook what those values are and how their jobs relate to each.

Brad Lynn, who was recently named a Star under the value of "Excite Every Fan," pulled some previously unpullable strings to allow two young local hockey teams to take a quick tour of the Marlies' locker room while the team was warming up on the ice. Unless you understand the position that hockey plays in Canadian culture, it might be hard to grasp what a big deal this is—but believe us, it is. Brad's ability to accommodate such a last-minute request gave a bunch of kids a memory of a lifetime.

"Moments of Truth"

What organizations like MLSE are trying to achieve is absolute clarity of purpose and direction for every single employee—and anyone else who's involved. They do it so that any staff member who encounters a moment of truth—be it a customer issue or opportunity, an operational emergency, or an ethical dilemma—can proceed on their own recognizance, guided by the beacon of knowledge that comes from understanding and really embracing the big picture.

In his book, *Moments of Truth*, former SAS Airline President Jan Carlzon suggested that these fleeting moments of interaction between customers and frontline employees determine the fate of any customer-driven organization. Speaking of SAS, he said, "If we are truly dedicated to orienting our company toward each customer's individual needs, then we cannot rely on rule books and instructions from distant corporate offices. We have to place responsibility for ideas, decisions, and actions with the people who are SAS during those brief seconds."[3] To be sure, Carlzon was not advocating that businesses be run purely on the whims of whatever each individual employee happens to feel like doing at the moment. Clearly, there needs to be some form of structure and a solid decision-making process. However, he *is* suggesting that the gulf that exists in many organizations between a truly involved workforce hitting on all cylinders and one that gives every appearance of being brain dead can be best bridged with credible information. As such, this insight must be artfully presented and continually reinforced in terms of where the organization is going, why it's going there, what it stands for, and what it needs and expects from all hands on deck. Good, timely information enables people to perform at a higher rate of speed and with fewer errors. If they don't have that information, they must inevitably slow down to sort things out.

As if to put a bow on the subject, Carlzon points out, "Setting a good example is truly the most effective means of communication, and setting a poor one is disastrous!"

High Expectations Beget High Performance

There is no middle ground when it comes to Commitment; people are either passengers or they're crew, Committed or they're not. If they fall into the latter category, it may not be because they're stupid, lazy, mean-spirited, or just plain "bad employees" (as much as you might want to believe otherwise). Okay, a few might be. But the main reason they perform the way they do is because we haven't done our part as leaders to get them enrolled in the journey.

To gain their support, we have to show them the big picture. According to Jack Stack, who brought Springfield Remanufacturing back from the brink, "The big picture is all about motivation. It's giving people the reason for doing the job, the purpose of working. If you're going to play a game, you have to understand what it means to win. When you show people the big picture, you define winning."[4]

Our firm's employee opinion surveys routinely question the extent to which respondents feel that upper management provides them ample information about the organization's goals. Seems like a fairly straightforward question, right? Well, the answer in the minds of more than 40 percent of the nearly 200,000 respondents over a 20-some-year period is—"They don't." Now, if you put any credence at all in Jack Stack's experience, this suggests that people have no hope whatsoever of winning in at least 40 percent of those cases. Face it: if we cannot or will not give our folks straightforward information about where the ship is headed, how can we possibly ask them to help us steer it?

High expectations create an environment where both individual and company growth can take place. Each and every one of us wants desperately to be a winner. However, people often don't know how to win in their jobs. Their managers have to show them or get used to the fact that everyone will lose while they stand idly by. Winning is too often defined in terms that are overly dry, sterile (take a look at your own company's strategic plans or "vision statements"), or completely irrelevant to the intended audience (Company X wants to achieve ROCE of 16.2 percent). It's time to get real! After all, Dr. Martin Luther King Jr. didn't launch an entire movement with the words "I have a strategic plan," did he?

Chapter Summary

1. Contented Cows are Committed Cows.

2. Employees won't part with their "discretionary effort" for just any old reason. They must have what they consider to be good and compelling reasons; the "cause" must be impeccably clear and compelling and must fit with their sensibilities.

3. Far too few employees know what the company does, where it's going, what it stands for, what it believes in, and where they fit in.

4. There's no middle ground when it comes to Commitment—you are either committed, or you aren't.

5. Committed employees are the only ones capable of delivering the kind of quality and service needed to compete and win.

6. Managers in Contented Cow companies communicate, through word and deed, and in every way imaginable, what the company is all about. The word *overcommunication* isn't even in their lexicon.

7. High expectations beget high performance.

CHAPTER
4

The Path to Commitment

When the organization has a clear sense of its purpose, direction, and desired future state, and when this image is widely shared, individuals are able to define their own roles both in the organization and the larger society of which they are a part. They gain a sense of importance as they are transformed from robots blindly following instructions to human beings engaged in a creative and purposeful venture.

—Warren Bennis and Burt Nanus, *Leaders*

So How Do You Get People Committed?

In an age when the on-ramp to the career expressway is shorter and steeper than ever (just ask Tim Tebow), forgiveness for mistakes is practically nonexistent, and the average job tenure is a little more than three years, it is imperative to get your employees up to speed quickly. That certainly includes enrolling them in the organization's journey before they get lost, run over—or just drop out.

There are four specific information needs you must meet as a prerequisite for achieving high levels of employee Commitment. In short, these are things your employees need, want, and have a right to know.

53

1. What Is This Organization All About?

Your people need to know what the organization stands for and what it believes in. What is really important? What kinds of things can they do to get support—or promoted? What will get them voted off the island? Because we all walk around with a healthy dose of skepticism these days, they also need to hear some stories that illustrate, validate, and anchor those claims, stories that involve heroes, villains, and victories snatched from the jaws of defeat by their coworkers.

No Identity Crisis at J&J

One organization that has demonstrated clear and consistent superiority in communicating its identity is Johnson & Johnson (J&J). In a short, 308-word document known simply as the Credo (http://www.jnj.com/connect/about-jnj/jnj-credo), they have effectively articulated just about everything anyone needs to know about what the company stands for and deems important. The Credo isn't something they cooked up just last week. It has been around about as long as their Band-Aids (since 1943, to be exact). Although it is subjected to regular internal review, they have hardly changed a word over that time. Indeed, in the 13 years since the original edition of this book was published, not one word of the Credo has been altered. Although many companies may have such hallowed documents stashed away in their vaults, it is doubtful that any could demonstrate as convincingly as J&J has that they actually mean it and believe what's printed on the paper.

J&J openly discusses their Credo with prospective employees, makes sure new hires get a copy of it, publishes it on the cover of their annual reports, and most important, they live it.

By his own admission, former J&J chief executive officer Jim Burke spent upward of 40 percent of his time communicating the Credo—not developing it, but *explaining* it. Although some might find it excessive for a CEO to spend that much of his or her time engaged in communicating what the organization stands for and where it's going, we would argue that it's the single most important job a CEO has!

According to Burke, "All of our management is geared to profit on a day-to-day basis. That's part of the business of being in business. But too often, in this and other businesses, people are inclined to think, 'We'd better do this, because it's going to show up on the figures over the short term.' This document allows them to say, 'Wait a minute. I don't *have* to do that. The management has told me that they're really interested in the long term, and they're interested in me operating under this set of principles. So I won't.'"[1]

Sellin' Chicken

The mission at Chick-fil-A is about as clear and uncomplicated as it gets. While I was conducting a Coaching Skills Workshop at the company's headquarters near the Atlanta airport, one class member volunteered that "[Founder and CEO] Truett Cathy has always been very clear about what we do here at Chick-fil-A: 'We sell chicken.' It's as simple as that. No matter what you're doing, if it pertains to sellin' chicken, then you're probably doing the right thing. If what you're doing gets in the way of sellin' chicken, or if it doesn't have anything to do with sellin' chicken, you better not let Truett find out about it. And he finds out about everything."

Truett Cathy never saw any reason to micromanage. He had been very clear for nearly 50 years and told his people in simple, easy-to-understand terms that as long as their activities promoted "sellin' chicken" (within the parameters of the company's unusually high standards of ethics and professionalism), they was sanctioned, condoned, and encouraged. That answered a lot of questions and eliminated the need for a lot of hefty policy manuals.

At one point in the workshop, I accompanied a small group from the class to a breakout room on another floor. As the elevator door opened, there stood Truett, on his way up to his office from the basement. After warm greetings to each of the seminar participants by name and an introduction to me, whom he didn't know, he asked interestedly, "Whatchall doin'?" They all chimed in chorus, "Sellin' chicken!" Truett beamed and probed no further.

Core Values on Display at Zappos

Online retailer Zappos operates by a list of Core Values (http://about .zappos.com/our-unique-culture/zappos-core-values), and it does a very effective job of making sure people understand and can live with them— both before and after they're hired.

I was initially a little skeptical of these claims. Then I took the Zappos tour and was amazed—not just by the degree to which the company really opens the kimono (nothing was off-limits), but by the extent to which the Core Values were on display, both in words and deeds. It was also refreshing to note that the very distinctive Zappos culture seems to have thus far survived their acquisition by Amazon.

Zappos was celebrating customer week while we were there. In mid-afternoon, the "normal" business environment was suddenly punctuated by a group of costumed workers parading through the cube farm, to the beat of loud music, passing out Jell-O shots (yes, Jell-O shots). By my count, at least three of their Core Values were on display that afternoon, to include #3 which involves "Creating fun and a little weirdness."

Subsequent to the tour, the company's values were put on display in a more somber way in early 2012, when they reacted quickly and in a very straightforward manner to a massive hack of their customer data files. The announcement to customers was lightning fast, crisp, and to the point: "We got hacked . . . we're sorry . . . here's what we have done . . . here's what you should probably do," etc. No lawyerly weasel words or obfuscation were involved, thereby satisfying Core Value #6, "Build open and honest relationships with communication."

> *I believe life is a series of near misses. A lot of what we ascribe to luck is not luck at all. It's seizing the day and accepting responsibility for your future. It's seeing what other people don't see and pursuing that vision.*
> —Howard Schultz, CEO of Starbucks

2. Where Are We Going, and Why?

People want to know what journey you are asking them to sign up for. Do you plan to go to the moon by the end of the decade? The White House in 2013? Achieve $10 billion in revenue by the year 2015? The World Cup championships in five years—or what? Sadly, most organizations fail miserably on this one. They either have no credible sense of mission, or they can't articulate it. Either way, it spells disaster.

If people don't know full well where your ship is headed, they can't possibly help you get there. Former General Electric (GE) CEO Jack

Welch said that a company must define its destiny in broad but clear terms: "You need an overarching message, something big, but simple and understandable."[2]

Former Southwest Airlines president and CEO Howard Putnam explained the very practical implications of the problem: "Most companies fail in their growth because they don't have a vision. They don't know where to go. When you have a vision and someone comes to you with some convoluted idea, you can hold it up to the vision and ask, does it fit? Does it fly? If not, don't bother me. A vision must be so strong that it can outweigh the egos of managers that might want to take off in a different direction."[3]

Lost in Space

Quick: What was the program goal of NASA's 135 space shuttle missions (launched over the course of 30 years at about $1.5 billion/copy)? What has been the goal of America's space program since 1969, when standing on the shoulders of their predecessors, the *Apollo 11* crew fulfilled President Kennedy's 1961 promise that Americans would put a man on the moon and return him safely to Earth before the end of the decade?

If the answers aren't coming to you quickly or clearly, don't feel bad. You are in good company, to include those members of Congress who vote to fund NASA, and even some at the agency itself. Is it really any wonder that America's space program as we have known it seems to be riding off into the sunset?

We discussed the eminent conclusion of NASA's shuttle program on our way to Titusville, Florida, to view the final shuttle launch in July 2011. In the pre-dawn darkness, some eight hours prior to the launch of *STS 135*, I hadn't yet sorted out my emotional reaction to the program's ending. However, what *was* clear is just how similar NASA's situation is to other entities (governments, companies, et al.) that lose their way, their funding, and their mojo.

The Bible's book of Proverbs 29:18 suggests that "where there is no vision, the people perish." This is yet another instance of an agency that has long operated with a very cloudy—or at best, misunderstood—sense of purpose, direction, and priority. It is one that is in real danger of going away, not because our nation has grown tired of space venture, but because of the persistent failure to clearly articulate a credible and compelling vision for the future.

The very same thing happens to companies, business units, departments, and teams that fail to credibly articulate and maintain a compelling sense of purpose and direction. As leaders, we must determine, communicate, and then permanently illuminate—with one of those big five-cell flash-lights—the path ahead. What are we about? Why does our organization exist? What is, as the French put it, our raison d'être? Where are we going? Why does it matter?

Fail to connect the dots on any one of these items and slowly (at first), but inexorably, the lights go out, and the party is over. A few suggestions:

- It is not enough once you've decided upon the "vision/mission thing" to simply announce it once or twice and then hang some relevant testimonial junk on the wall. To overcome the understandable cynicism that exists inside organizations, we need to practically litter the place with repeated signs that this is *much* more than some new program. Rather, it is to be our way of life. Words are important, but actions trump syllables.

- To breathe life into those words and make them part of our daily actions, we should make it clear to the people on our team that good faith efforts on their part to enact the vision will never get them in trouble. Similarly, they should stop doing anything that does not line up with that purpose as soon as practical. On an institutional level, we must take pains to be sure that budgets and reward mechanisms support our declared purpose and direction.

- To be sure, Level 1 and 2 managers (those closest to the front line, and the ones with the toughest jobs in any organization) are responsible for ensuring that their teammates get the big picture. But because people don't operate day to day in the big picture, they must see to it that those around them clearly grasp the top two or three priorities.

The "Crayon Test"

In his book *Beating the Street*, former Fidelity Magellan Fund manager Peter Lynch makes the case that investors ought not put their money into anything that cannot be explained with a crayon.[4] Given the complexity of today's financial markets, that's probably good advice. It is every bit as useful, however, for those of us who are entrusted with the responsibility of explaining to others where our organization is headed. If you can't convey that message, graphically and credibly, with the very same crayon (literally), then you can't explain it and your people ought not (and probably won't) invest in it!

Once you've made the journey and its purpose impeccably clear, however, it's time for everyone (no exceptions) to either enthusiastically get in the boat and start rowing or be thrown overboard. As the late David Packard of HP fame pointed out, "There can be no place for half-hearted interest or effort . . . A high degree of enthusiasm should be encouraged at all levels; in particular, the people in high management positions must not only be enthusiastic themselves, but they must be able to engender enthusiasm among their associates."[5]

3. How Do We Plan to Get There?

The process an organization uses to determine its destination is far less important than the methods it uses to communicate it and the level of discipline it employs to get and keep people moving in the same direction. After the destination becomes clear, people have a right to know how you intend to get there. What's the game plan for achieving your destination? Although you don't need to lay out the entire plan—in fact, you are probably better off if there's a little room for improvisation—clarifying the first two or three steps would be a great start.

Play Scripting

Many National Football League (NFL) teams today use a practice first developed by former San Francisco 49ers head coach Bill Walsh called play scripting. On the day before a game, coaches simply make a list of the first 10 or 12 offensive plays the team will run the next day, and then they share the list with players in their Saturday night meeting. According to Walsh, players like it because it eliminates some pregame anxiety by allowing them to know ahead of time what they'll be doing on the first few series and giving them a chance to think about and visualize it. Some might even sleep better.[6] The benefits for young first- and second-year players are immense; it helps them compartmentalize their responsibilities at a time when they are still trying to master a very fast game. Sound familiar?

And we could all do worse than achieve Walsh-like results. In 10 seasons under Walsh, the 49ers won three Super Bowls and six NFL Western Division titles.

4. How Do I Fit In?

Finally, people need to know what role you want them to play and what it is you'll be expecting of them. We made the point earlier that you've got to get the big picture indelibly burned into your employees' gray matter. And you do. But people don't work day to day in the big picture. Instead, the proof is in the details, which—individually and taken together—send powerful messages that either confirm and support or contradict the big picture.

As organizations get larger, it's virtually inevitable that people will begin to lose sight of where they fit in and how their contribution matters. Without regular and vigorous reinforcement on this point, many employees ultimately reach the conclusion that their contributions really don't matter all that much, and the decline in their effort is at hand. People who have come to believe that their role isn't all that important fail to shout "stop" when they discover a defective product or process or when a disgruntled customer walks out the door—and they definitely don't hustle.

We all want to be a part of something important and to play a meaningful role. Imagine for a moment how difficult it would be for you to remain Committed to something if you were at all uncertain about whether or not your efforts really mattered. We're often reminded of this point whenever there's a snowstorm of any size in our nation's capital, and the airwaves are immediately filled with announcements for government employees that only people in essential positions need report for work. Now, deep down, who in the world wants something they spend 8 hours a day doing to be deemed "nonessential"?

The nanosecond your people feel that it's no longer important for them to do their very best work, your company has started down a very steep and slippery slope. Sorry for the replay, but the point bears repeating: "High expectations breed high performance."

If you are working on something exciting that you really care about, you don't have to be pushed. The vision pulls you.

—Steve Jobs

Chapter Summary

1. Commitment starts with knowing the big picture and answering the following questions:

   o What is this company all about?

   o Where are we going, and why?

   o How do we plan to get there?

   o How do I fit in?

2. You've got to be able to articulate it simply and credibly. Remember the crayons!

Contented Cows
Are Cared About

CHAPTER 5

First You Feed the Troops

I sincerely believe that to be a successful commander, you must care.
—Major General Melvin Zais, U.S. Army

On a bleak and windy night on the remote island of Orkney off the northern coast of Scotland, Sergeant Major Jim Prentice of the Gordon Highlanders—a Scottish regiment of the British Army—was leading 36 soldiers in maneuvers to prepare for the World War II battles soon to come in far-off Burma. A sudden snowstorm had made it too dangerous to return to their camp, so Prentice enlisted the hospitality of the nearest farmhouse's inhabitants to provide a place for his men to sleep in the adjacent barn.

Happy to help, the farmer insisted that the soldiers be fed before retiring for the night. He and his family prepared an inelegant feast of ground beef, potatoes, turnips, carrots, and pancakes. Six at a time, the soldiers warmed themselves and filled their insides in the modest farmhouse's kitchen, while the others waited appreciatively in the barn.

The farmer's nine-year-old son watched curiously as Prentice, obviously the ranking soldier among them, ushered each sextet into the house. Only when all the troops had been served did the sergeant major sit down and eat. Curious at this unexpected behavior, the boy, who had been invited by the sergeant major to join him at the rough-hewn table, asked, "Why'd you go last? You're the leader!"

Prentice looked the young man in the eye and said with both conviction and instruction, "Lad, first you feed the troops. They're no good to you hungry."

It was a maxim by which Prentice led his troops through more than three hellish years in the Southeast Asian jungle and which he later credited for their safe return to Scotland. After the war, again using the philosophy that "first you feed the troops," he built a successful commercial construction company in Scotland's Clyde Valley region.

No softie, Jim Prentice was a pragmatic business owner with an eighth grade education who knew how to get the most from people—both on the battlefield and the building site. He knew what the leaders of Contented Cows know: first you feed the troops. They're no good to you hungry.

You Can't Fake Caring

Let's first establish the fact that caring is not a program, a technique, or something that can be taught or bought. It's not a quid pro quo, nor does it require you to coddle people, make them feel "comfortable," or provide false hope or security.

Your team members are a lot more rational than they get credit for. They really don't expect a "free ride." They know that you can't insulate them from anxiety and job stress any more than their homeowner's policy can keep a hurricane from roaring through their neighborhood. They also know that you really can't guarantee their job security. But they do expect you to be fiercely Committed to things like being scrupulously honest with them, believing in them, helping them succeed, and being there for them when they need it—and rightfully so. They know that when push comes to shove, you either care or you don't, and that nobody is a good enough actor to fake it for long.

According to legendary former Los Angeles Dodgers manager Tommy Lasorda, a wise manager goes out of his or her way to let people know how important they are on a regular basis. As Lasorda explained, "I want my players to know that I appreciate what they do for me [and] that I depend on them. When you, as a leader of people, are naive enough to think that you, not your players, won the game, then you're in bad shape."[1] This is doubtlessly one of the reasons Lasorda was frequently the first one out of the dugout to congratulate his players for making a big play.

The Best of All Worlds at Incepture

Earnie Franklin, CEO of Jacksonville-based staffing company Incepture, beams every time he talks about the team he's led over the past five years.

What began as a vertically integrated staffing function for Blue Cross and Blue Shield of Florida has evolved into a leading provider of contract staff in the health care and technology sectors. Incepture was also named one of *Florida Trend* magazine's "Best Companies to Work For" in 2011 and one of the *Jacksonville Business Journal's* "Best Places to Work" for the same year.

When Franklin took the helm in 2007, he wanted to create a place that combined the best of all the worlds in which he'd worked before, while omitting all the bad stuff. After spending most of his career in big corporate settings, he got the chance to run TriServe Alliance, a small entrepreneurial company that provides health care services to the U.S. Armed Forces.

"All the weight of the corporate bureaucracy had been lifted off me [when I began at TriServe]," Franklin told us. "One day, a friend with whom I was having lunch said he noticed a real difference in me. He said I seemed happier, more enthusiastic, and really excited about what we were doing. And I *was*. We had the freedom there to make decisions by *information*, not politics, or committee. People would come to work there and say, 'Wow! This is great!'"

"I'd been both in the big companies, and now in an agile, flexible setting, and I knew which one I did better work in," he added.

So when the opportunity arose for Franklin to take over Incepture, he knew exactly what he would do. He'd combine the processes, structure, and logistical thinking of his corporate experience with the people orientation of an entrepreneurial company and turn it into a mission-based company where people could pursue what they wanted to be—both professionally and personally. "I was convinced we could do that and still make money. And I don't have to tell *you* this," he winked, "but I was right."

"The more you genuinely care about the people you work with, the better," he went on to say. "At one point, I got confused about how close you can get with people at work, especially if you're in a leadership role. You can't become their best friend. It's not like that. But at least here, with our size, it *is* like family, in a sense."

"I always want people to feel they can come and talk to me. So as a part of my business strategy, I intentionally spend a lot of time with the people who work here. I talk to them, and mentor some of them, because I learn so much from them when I do. It really is a lot more about the people you lead than it is the leader."

Something about Franklin's philosophy and practices seems to resound both with employees and with clients. Since 2008, in the midst of a soft labor market, the company has more than doubled its contractor placements.

> *I feel that you have to be with your employees through all their difficulties, that you have to be interested in them personally. I want them to know that Southwest will always be there for them.*
>
> —Herb Kelleher, cofounder, chairman emeritus,
> Southwest Airlines

Delta's Gerald Grinstein—A Class Act

Workers understand the concept that senior executives earn more than worker bees, but there's a multiple at which the "caring" argument loses credibility. As Delta Air Lines CEO from 2004 to 2007, Gerald Grinstein led the Atlanta-based carrier through bankruptcy and has been more or less universally credited with its successful reincarnation. In 2005, he took a self-imposed 25 percent pay cut to an annual salary of $338,000 which was less than the salaries of some of his subordinates, and substantially lower than the pay of peers at some of Delta's equally beleaguered competitors. "There has to be restraint on the part of management," Grinstein said. "Everybody has made sacrifices, and incentives for management can't sound excessive."[2] Upon Delta's exit from bankruptcy protection in April 2007, Grinstein declined the postbankruptcy bonus to which he was entitled. He instructed that the $10 million amount be used instead to fund scholarships and emergency hardship assistance for Delta employees, families, and retirees.

The day after Delta's emergence, I had the occasion to speak with and congratulate several of their employees while traveling to Atlanta for a meeting. In separate conversations, two of these people volunteered that had it not been for Grinstein's leadership, they doubted the bankruptcy would have ended when it did, if at all. Each of them brought up Grinstein's refused bonus, and one man remarked, "I would follow him to hell and back."

A May 18, 2007, piece in *USA Today* noted that Mr. Grinstein's counterparts at United and Northwest (both also recently bankrupt) had apparently decided to be a little (make that a lot) less magnanimous with their own postemergence party favors. The article went on to note the presence of angry employees at two of the aforementioned airlines. Wanna guess which two?

Caring is not a photo-op. Rather, it's an attitude reflected by personal and organizational priorities. Organizations that care about their people take pains to ensure that human considerations are in the forefront of their decision-making process, whether developing corporate programs and policies; acquiring and designing facilities, equipment, and systems; or scheduling and arranging work. This is not something they do some of the time, or most of the time, but *always*—even when it's unpopular or seemingly less profitable to do so.

An organization's degree of caring is evidenced not by what it says but by what it does. After all, what rational company would claim not to care?

R-E-S-P-E-C-T at Plantronics Mexico

When Alejandro Bustamante assumed the role of president of Plamex, the Mexican division of headset maker Plantronics, in the mid-1990s, he encountered a largely disaffected workforce in a factory struggling to meet the demands of a growing market fueled by rapidly changing technology. Quickly assessing the situation he'd walked into, Bustamante determined that he couldn't fundamentally change anyone, but what he *could* do was institute a culture in which everyone—*everyone*—was treated with respect. He soon restored respect and a real sense of dignity in the plant, and as a result, he and his team have pulled off a business turnaround of gigantic proportion. The company's output, quality, profitability, and reputation as *the* place to work in Mexico have all soared.

"The job of a leader," he told me, while standing in the entrance to the Tijuana facility's large main factory, "is to create the atmosphere to get the results we want. It's as simple as that. It's not always easy to *do*, but it's not complicated."

When I asked Bustamante to explain how Plamex had gone from its 1995 state to being named the number one Best Place to Work in all of Mexico by the Great Place to Work Institute in 2011, the Tijuana native had a ready answer:

> *There are three things we want for every one of our 2,286 associates here. First, we want to give everyone the respect they deserve. Second, we want to develop each one of them, to let them do as much as they want and go as far as they want. And third—and this is probably the most important—we want to improve the quality of their lives, and the lives of their families. When you do those things, you get their very best. And that's what we need—their very best.*

Making telephone headsets is a labor-intensive process. And even in an area populated by more than 2 million people, it's long been difficult to find enough skilled workers to staff the many maquiladoras in the Free Trade Zone area of Tijuana. The Plamex workforce is comprised of about 20 percent locals and a whopping 80 percent who come from other states in the interior of Mexico. Many employers in the area spend heavily on recruiting, owing in part to the talent shortage and exacerbated by working conditions that lead to high turnover. But not at Plamex.

It's the Little Things . . . Always the Little Things

As an early demonstration of respect, Bustamante had business cards printed for and distributed to *every* worker in the factory, cards that they proudly showed to family and friends in their communities. Soon, as a direct result of the business cards, this "badge of honor," as his associates saw it, his HR department had more applicants than they could hire, coming from all over the country. A nearby factory manager complained to Bustamante that Plamex was getting all the good workers and that he couldn't compete because he couldn't spend the money, as Plamex had, to print business cards for everybody.

"How much do you spend every year on advertising and recruiting?" Bustamante asked his neighbor.

"About $200,000" was the reply.

"Spend a few hundred instead on business cards, and then we'll be on a level playing field," Bustamante told him.

A New Take on "Employee Engagement" Whoda Thunk It?

My visit to Plamex in Tijuana revealed more than we have room to share here about the striking results that stem from overtly caring about your workforce. One of the most remarkable parts of the Plamex culture, and one that illustrates the importance of family at Plamex, is their unconventional practice of hosting employee weddings on-site.

Until recently, Mexican couples desiring a marriage license were required to produce their original birth certificates, which could be obtained only by making a pilgrimage to the town of their birth. As 80 percent of Plamex's workforce is nonlocal, this presented a logistical nightmare for most. As a result, many couples who *wanted* to marry simply couldn't. Yet, being together out of wedlock presented an awkward dilemma for some on both social and religious grounds. To help with the problem, Plamex began granting associates time off to retrieve their documentation. A number of employees made use of the privilege.

Bustamante decided it might be nice to actually host a mass wedding, uniting the couples right there in the plant. He negotiated a special discounted license fee with local authorities and even convinced a judge to mass produce the nuptials for the price of a single wedding. (It is a factory, after all. ☺) Plamex associates provided the food, music, and decorations, and Bustamante opened the factory's capacious dining hall for the festivities.

After the first group wedding, which was an unqualified success, two teenagers, a brother and sister, came up to him and said, "Mr. Bustamante, thank you so much for doing this. We are so proud that our parents are now able to be married."

"That's all it took," Bustamante told me, "and I knew we were doing a good thing."

Plamex lobbied the Mexican government to change the law, and now getting a marriage license no longer requires a trek home. Still, the weddings were such a hit that the practice continues. Every year around Valentine's Day, the company hosts a mass wedding of some 20 to 30 couples, at least one member of which is a Plamex associate. Total cost to Plamex for each event: about $300. This practice, along with so many others that make up the way of life at Plamex, helps fulfill the organization's goal of optimizing business outcomes by first demonstrating in tangible ways that they truly care about workers.

A leader should possess human understanding and consideration for others. Men are not robots and should not be treated as such. I do not by any means suggest coddling. But men are intelligent, complicated beings who will respond favorably to human understanding and consideration. By these means their leader will get maximum effort from each of them. He will also get loyalty.

—General Omar Bradley

Order Up

For years, my office in Jacksonville was across a busy street from a place called The Sandwich Store, a little nondescript eatery owned and operated by Renee Curry. The food was good—very good, in fact—but what was really impressive was the speed with which Curry and her three coworkers could make a sandwich, fill a soft drink cup, ring up the order, get it all correct, and get people on their way—and the fact that they did this somewhere between 300 and 400 times every day!

These folks (the same three employees for years, I hasten to add) were focused like a laser on that objective. They executed so well that we would highly recommend the place to the industrial engineers at McDonald's and Burger King who could no doubt learn a thing or two.

One reason that Curry was able to keep the same folks making her "Incredible Roast Beef Creations" and frying frozen potatoes for so long is that she cared about those often nameless faces who fed the masses each day. "These are the people who are making me money!" she shrieked at me as though it should be obvious, and she was right. Curry lent her employees money when they were in a pinch (which wasn't often), and not one ever abused her kindness. They all had their evenings free, so at least three times a year she would take the crew out to dinner. They earned paid vacation—in a sandwich shop! And during the Christmas season, she put up a little tree, like a special holiday tip jar, to which many appreciative customers paper clipped "gifts." (Who says money doesn't grow on trees?)

"I care about them, and they care about me, and about each other. It's great," said this strong businesswoman with a personality that doesn't suffer slackers lightly. She once offered an employee the extra bedroom in her house, rent free. Did she feel that she had a social obligation to take in the down-and-out? No, Curry told me, "It's because she was a damn good worker, and I knew that she'd be at work every day if she had a place to stay that was nearby. I was right, and she made us both a bunch of money."

Safety Is No Accident at Alaska Clean Seas

Concurrent with the belief that workers are, in the words of Jim Prentice, "no good to you hungry" is the recognition that people can't work as well (or at all) if they're hurt (or worse).

No sensible person would argue the merits of a safe workplace. Most of its benefits are self-evident. There are other benefits, however, that are less obvious, but no less significant. Workers who have to spend one nanosecond worrying about their own safety, or who have to make cumbersome adjustments to their work in order to stay out of harm's way, can't possibly give their full measure of effort. They've got to slow down—beyond the reasonable slowdown that comes with giving due care to the job.

Let's be clear: safety is *everyone's* job. It's the leader's job to be sure that everyone knows that.

When leaders show (as opposed to merely mouthing the words) that safety is a big deal, they demonstrate in a clear and compelling way that they *care* about their followers. And take this to the bank: we know that people absolutely, positively reserve their best effort for leaders who care about them as humans.

Safety is an integral part of caring.

One of the more unique projects we've worked on was with Alaska Clean Seas (ACS), an oil spill response organization with offices in Anchorage and operations in the North Slope oil fields, 300 miles inside the Arctic Circle.

As you might imagine, the risks involved with cleaning up oil spills—even tiny ones—in the frozen tundra and icy waters, in temperatures that commonly dip to more than 40 degrees below zero Fahrenheit (which also happens to be $-40°C$) are formidable. As a result, there's a pervasive—some would say obsessive—emphasis on safety in the ACS culture.

The conditions on the Slope also drive the unique work schedule that, although typical in the world of oil drilling (and the work that supports it), is unusual for the rest of us. These folks, like most Slope employees, work a two-week "hitch" of 14 straight 12-hour days and then fly home (wherever home might be, often outside the state), where they can do whatever they like before flying back up for their next hitch two weeks later.

In January (brr!) 2011, I visited ACS's Prudhoe Bay operation in preparation for the event we facilitated the following April in Anchorage. Before leaving for the aptly named Deadhorse Airport, I was fed constant reminders of how thoroughly safety is woven into everything on the Slope and at ACS. I was required to wear special clothing, including special shoes, before they would allow me to board the shared service flight that ferries oil workers from Alaska's largest city to its northernmost region. An ACS representative met me in Deadhorse, issued safety goggles and a hard hat before getting into the truck, and reminded me to fasten my seat belt. Later, I was caught not holding onto the handrail when boarding the company minibus and my behavior was corrected.

Although every ACS worker I encountered made me highly safety-conscious, the issue of safety has no greater champion at ACS than president and general manager Ron Morris—who eats, breathes, and lives safety. I guess I was a slow learner when it came to the handrail thing, because even in the relatively safe confines of the camp's living facilities, Morris was talking casually with me and stopped midsentence as we ascended a flight of stairs to interject, "Handrail, please." He didn't apologize, but he did explain: "It's a reflex. It's just baked into me."

ACS holds safety meetings once a week. Although this isn't unusual in industrial settings, the one I attended on radon contamination in the home demonstrated how much ACS cares about workers' safety both on the Slope and off through its Taking Safety Home program. ACS not only includes safety incentives in its bonus plan, but an employee who participates in a safety presentation earns points toward the annual bonus. Every year, if at least 50 percent of the company's employees participate in conducting a presentation at a safety meeting, more money gets thrown into the shared bonus pot.

What's been the effect of this unrelenting focus on safety at ACS? The event for which they brought us to Anchorage in April was, among other things, a celebration of a remarkable milestone: 10 years without a single lost-time accident . . . *10 years!* Take just a moment to let that sink in—an entire decade with more than 3 million worker hours, and no lost-time accidents. That's impressive for even the least hazardous of office environments, but under the conditions inherent in ACS's work, it's incredible!

An achievement such as this doesn't happen by . . . well . . . by accident. It happens only through leadership and a Commitment by everyone in the company.

One distinguishing feature of ACS's emphasis on safety is its Behavior-Based Safety Process, the objective of which is to change behavior, not necessarily the person. Certified peer observers (no managers allowed) evaluate workers performing tasks associated with their jobs and describe the behaviors they observe in terms of "safes" and "at-risks." What's somewhat remarkable is that they conduct these checks with the worker's full knowledge *and* permission. The process's success derives in part from its nonconfrontational and nonpunitive nature—one that is founded on education, not reprimand. The results of the observation are documented, but without identifying anyone by name or gender.

"It's not so important to know who did what," said Emily McBride, a warehouse lead in charge of the program, "only to learn from what we've observed."

Safety is so much a part of ACS that we weren't surprised when Ron Morris opened the Anchorage meeting—held on the 10th floor of the Captain Cook Hotel—with a safety briefing. Having already checked out the emergency exits personally, Morris let us all know how to escape in the event of fire, earthquake, or anything else that makes outside look better than inside. The fact that we were meeting in a hotel that was built directly on the site and in the immediate aftermath of one of the strongest quakes ever recorded on Earth certainly made this Florida boy sit up and listen.

One element of the Anchorage event was a video we produced that featured ACS employees, and in a few cases, their family members. "It's all about getting home to my family every two weeks," one long-term spill technician told the camera. One of the wives, referring to the fact that these workers are paid handsomely for this less-than-cushy job, mentioned that no amount of money was worth having to worry every time her husband went up for his hitch. She expressed her appreciation to the company's leadership for making safety such a paramount priority.

Although cynics might claim that this emphasis on safety is based more on a healthy fear of lawsuits and Occupational Safety and Health Administration (OSHA) regulations than on a genuine sense of caring about people, a single visit to ACS in Deadhorse, Alaska, would swiftly alter that perspective.

Later in the year, we keynoted Graycor Industrial Constructors, Inc.'s Annual Safety Boot Camp. The sole reason for this gathering of company managers was to showcase the importance of safety, continue to reinforce the company's standards, and provide additional practical training in the how-to's of safety.

The message from Graycor's leaders, although not in these exact words, was crystal clear: "We're serious about safety. We want (and expect) you to take it seriously as well. We're not going to go wink-wink-nod-nod when you don't do little things by the book. And if you commit, or allow others to commit unsafe practices—either by your permission or your silence—we're going to show you what else hammers can be used for."

That, too, is caring.

So, leaders, if you care about your people—which of course means caring about their safety—here are a few to-do's to ensure you're executing your leadership responsibilities in that regard:

- Mind yourself first. Model safety in all you do—both at work and away. Use seat belts, helmets, and handrails; drive well; operate machines correctly; and make smart moves—whatever means safety in your world.

- Keep your eyes and ears open for hazards, especially of the not-so-obvious variety.

- Keep your mind open to suggestions from others about potential hazards and ways to make your workplace safer.

- Develop methods and processes that encourage safety awareness, and make it easy to comply with them. Be sure people fully understand the consequences of carelessness.

- Learn about, then consider implementing, a behavior-based safety program.

- Be like the folks at Graycor—totally unambiguous about your standards with regard to safety issues.

- Emulate our friends at Alaska Clean Seas: celebrate your success with respect to safety, but never grow complacent.

Motivation Doesn't Necessarily Follow Money

Let's take time out right now to debunk a fairly popular myth: caring about your people *does not* mean lavishing them with money and expensive benefits or increases and extras that they haven't earned, the market doesn't require, and you can't afford. U.S. automakers and airlines are but two examples of industries that have been guilty of all three of these activities in their pattern of frequent capitulations to their respective labor unions. Absent compelling reasons for these actions, the companies in these sectors have, over their long histories, done themselves and their employees (not to mention customers and shareholders) a huge disservice—and everyone involved knew it. Not unlike a "one night stand," it may have felt good at the time, but they've been paying for it ever since.

People don't care how much you know until they know how much you care.
—Anonymous

It wouldn't have taken an economic genius to see the June 2009 eventual undoing of General Motors coming—a failure that resulted in the fourth largest bankruptcy filing in American history. We actually predicted the company's demise in the first version of this book when we chronicled its downward spiral through the decades of the 1980s and 1990s, on the backs of the same ills that brought it to its knees in the first decade of the new millennium. And the ability of the company's leadership to right the listing ship appeared not to have improved one iota since then GM boss Roger Smith said, in 1993, "I don't know. It's a mysterious thing," when asked to explain what had happened.[3]

It's a mystery to us how Smith could claim *not* to know. One need only look at GM's share of the U.S. car market and their market value to realize that something went seriously wrong. That share slid from 32 percent to 19.6 percent between 1995 and 2011, and the company's market value plummeted from $56 billion in 2000 to about $7 billion by 2008.[4] The world's largest automaker, once a behemoth of industry on the world stage was, at that point, worth about half as much as cosmetics company Avon.[5]

By providing "benefits" such as fully funded, zero-deductible health, vision, and dental care and supplemental unemployment insurance, GM had ratcheted its production labor costs into the $40 per hour vicinity by early 1996. By 2008, it was a staggering $73.26 per hour![6]—juxtaposed against a comparable rate at Toyota of about $48 per hour in its older U.S. plants and less than that in newer ones. Now, you've got to be pretty good to give your competitors a $25 an hour head start and *still* expect to beat them in the marketplace. It would seem that someone might have deduced that something was terribly amiss when the cost of "benefits" started exceeding the cost of the steel needed to make cars. Yet no one did. And between 2005 and mid-2009, General Motors managed somehow to lose an unfathomable $88 billion![7]

Although admittedly a matter of opinion, we happen to believe that the problems at GM had far more to do with worker attitudes and commitment level (demoralized by an inattentive and uncaring management and a fractious relationship with the United Auto Workers union) than with engineering, design, marketing, finance, or manufacturing processes. Think about it: GM enjoyed a huge brand name advantage, employed some of the best designers and marketing minds on the planet, and had spent enough of their capital reserves on technological improvement to have bought Toyota outright . . . and yet they were still making crummy cars! Go figure.

Just who benefits when GM is forced to close 14 plants and three distribution warehouses; when more than 20,000 people, most with families to support, lose their jobs and ways of life; when the U.S. government has to bail the company out to the tune of $52 billion; and when that same government still, as of this writing, owns a substantial portion of the company?

In our view, two of the most uncaring things you can do to people are (1) to give them something—whether they've earned it or not—knowing full well you'll have to ask for it back and (2) to blow smoke up their noses (or other bodily orifices). How do you think *your* people see it?

In fact, we submit that inordinately high wages, salaries, and unwarranted benefits not only *aren't* the answer but that they are often a large part of the problem. Moreover, companies often use or view them as a way to counterbalance or compensate for serious deficiencies elsewhere. Granted, no organization can expect to maintain esprit de corps by paying substandard salaries, but a lot of damage is done when people see money being thrown around. Once this occurs, pay loses its meaning, because people assume that the money must have been easy to get. They know they're not worth that much. Remuneration loses its relevance and impact, like a Christmas morning when all the presents under the tree have your name on them.

Money will not necessarily buy you a peak performing organization either. An analysis of team payrolls versus team performance in the 2009–2010 National Football League (NFL) season shows that by and large, money did not predict success. In fact, some of the winningest teams in the NFL had among the lowest payrolls, and vice versa. Further to the point that motivation doesn't necessarily follow money:

1. Of the 10 teams with the highest payrolls, only 3 finished the season in the top 10.
2. The highest-paid team finished smack in the middle of the rankings, with an 8 and 8 record.
3. The seventh ranked team had the fifth lowest payroll.

4. Only half of the top 50 percent in pay even managed a winning season.

·5. Just one of the top 5 paying teams even made the playoffs.

As George Steinbrenner, legendary New York Yankees owner learned, although it does take money to acquire and retain the best players, a fat payroll in no way guarantees team performance.

Google Is Great—But It's Not for Everybody

One of the first questions we ask when conducting a leadership seminar is, "What are some organizations that you *believe* would be great to work for?" Neither of us can recall asking that question in the past five years and having Google *not* make the list.

This isn't surprising. When it comes to lists, Google seems to be ever present, topping the *Fortune* "Best Places to Work" list in 2007, 2008, and again in 2012, and holding the not-too-shabby number 4 slot in the intervening years. Almost everyone who follows workplace issues (and many who don't) have heard of the legendary perks: free gourmet meals, all day, every day; yoga classes; in-house doctors; dry cleaning; massage service; swimming pool; and even hi-tech Wi-Fi-equipped biodiesel buses that transport workers to and from the company's Mountain View, California, headquarters. (See more on Google's benefits in Chapter 9.)

And who *wouldn't* be attracted to and excited by these creature comforts? But since there's more (much more) to a job than the things you do when you're not actually working, we were *not* surprised to learn that, in fact, Google *is* a fantastic and highly fulfilling workplace—that is, for a relatively narrow band of people. To the company's credit, they've learned (for the most part) how to select from the 1 million-plus applicants they receive each year, only those people who—by virtue of both talent *and* temperament—have the potential to be happy, productive, and successful working at Google—a company with a well-defined and highly uncommon culture.

At Google, it's not just about feeding your face at any time of the day but also about feeding your passion for creativity and innovation and solving challenges our parents wouldn't even have *thought* of. Let's be honest; they're challenges most of *us* wouldn't have thought of.

Googlers, as the company's employees call themselves, work hard—very hard. And they're expected to meet some very high standards. Laboring with an inventor's fervor and focus, they often put in seemingly interminable hours, working on such cool stuff that most report that they hardly even notice . . . while they're working anyway.

If you enjoy having people listen to and consider your creative ideas, working at Google might be for you. If you have a need for structure in your workday and around your schedule, then it's likely not the place for you. If you like working with truly brilliant thinkers, Google is likely to turn you on. For those with lots of outside responsibilities or interests—a high-maintenance family situation, time-consuming pastimes or hobbies—a Google job is something you'll probably only read about.

If you do better in low-pressure, routine environments, then you'd do better to look elsewhere. But if you thrive on doing work that has well-above-average *impact*, then you'd probably fall in love with Google work. We say impact because Google—whether it be the ubiquitous search tool or one or more of their other products (Docs, Maps, Gmail, Translate, Voice, YouTube, you name it)—has become an immeasurable part of life in almost every corner of the developed world. Indeed, this book was written on Google Docs. Just as it's hard for us to imagine the world without the Internet, it's hard to imagine the Internet without Google.

And it's hard to imagine achieving Google's success without attracting and retaining the kinds of people they need to fuel their engine. Hell, a *single share* of their stock is more than I paid for either of my first two cars!

Google's ability to massage its workers' creative juices—even more than their achy shoulder muscles—is what differentiates their employer brand from that of its competitors for highly specialized talent. And this is a resource that, even in periods of high unemployment, is too scarce to satisfy its demand.

Reason #4 on Google's Top Ten Reasons to Work at Google: Work and play are not mutually exclusive. It is possible to code and pass the puck at the same time.

Pebble Beach Company—If You Care, You Listen

Like thousands of other organizations, the Pebble Beach Company (PBC)—operator of the famous golf resort on California's Monterey Peninsula—performs periodic employee engagement surveys. What they know that a lot of others don't grasp, however, is that such surveys, well used, are an opportunity to listen—really listen to their workforce. And indeed listening is one of the foremost ingredients of caring.

It's been our firm's privilege to manage their survey projects since 2004. Unlike so many other companies, Pebble Beach management doesn't just ask the questions, tabulate the results, and then go back to sleep. They listen, they learn, they take the results seriously, and actually *do* something with them.

On a recent trip to Pebble Beach to discuss the results of the just-completed survey, we were only a little surprised when CEO Bill Perocchi began rattling off—from memory and with incredible precision—specific results from a survey they'd conducted *six years earlier!*

Okay, maybe that's not so surprising for a former General Electric auditor like Perocchi. But what *is* worth more than mentioning is that the company makes strategic use of its survey results in managing its business—and we'd advise you to do the same if you're going to do a survey. It's but one of the many inputs that PBC uses to determine leadership assignments, coaching opportunities, and investment in employee benefits and programs. Perhaps most important, it speaks to how the company is doing in managing its *culture*, that elusive but oh-so-visible quality that keeps guests returning to this special place by the sea.

> *We've all heard the criticism he talks too much. When was the last time you heard someone criticized for listening too much?*
>
> —Norm Augustine

Chapter Summary

1. Caring is an attitude, not a program. It has nothing whatsoever to do with sentiment, emotions, or "being nice."
2. First you feed the troops.

3. Caring can't be faked.

4. Safety is an integral part of caring.

5. Motivation doesn't necessarily follow money.

6. Perks, benefits, and amenities don't begin to tell the whole story of what makes a great workplace.

Better Practices:

1. Graycor's Safety Boot Camp and Alaska Clean Seas's behavior-based safety program

2. Business cards for *everyone* at Plamex

3. Pebble Beach's use of employee engagement survey results

CHAPTER

6

Tell 'Em the Truth

We adopted a philosophy that we wouldn't hide anything, not any of our problems, from the employees.

—Rollin King, founder of Southwest Airlines

Truth or Consequences

Few things abound within the employment arena that are more poisonous than insincerities, half-truths, insidious omissions, and just plain lies. One of the principal reasons the truly great companies find themselves atop the summit of success year after year is because they go to great lengths to avoid confusing people by lying to them, particularly those people who are or aspire to be on their payroll.

If you care about your people, you make it a point to tell them the truth, even when—in fact, *especially* when—it hurts. Good leaders endure personal discomfort to deliver bad news in an up close and personal way.

I once had a conversation with Dennis LeStrange, then a business unit leader with IKON Office Solutions (a Ricoh company) immediately after his return from a meeting in which he had informed a group of employees that their office was being shuttered. Admitting that it was a difficult meeting and that he could easily have sent a subordinate manager to handle the task, he recognized that people needed to hear the bad news quickly rather than read it in an e-mail or hear about it on TV—and that they deserved to hear it directly from the person who had made the decision.

Frequent flyers share a universal perspective on flight delays and other travel disruptions to which too many airline personnel seem oblivious. We know that pilots can't control the weather any more than gate agents can influence crowded runways or flight attendants can prevent a hydraulic problem from grounding the flight upon which we were desperately counting to get us home. But we do ask for the truth—in enough time to be of value.

Like many of you, we get to work by air many days, and we've noticed—especially in the past couple of years—a concerted and deliberate effort on the part of the people of Delta Air Lines (the carrier we fly most often) to provide passengers with more timely, truthful information. When they're on their game (which isn't every time, but often), they're likely to tell us:

- What's going on
- What they think's going to happen as a result
- Their best estimate of when we'll be on our way
- When they'll get back to us with more information

That's all we ask. And it's all that most reasonable people who look to you for leadership at work ask as well.

A Truth Recession

No period in recent history is more teeming with examples of the failure to tell the truth than that associated with the global financial crisis of the late 2000s and the great recession that followed. A prominent member of the United States Congress told the nation that mortgage giants Fannie Mae and Freddie Mac were "fundamentally sound" and "not in a crisis," when he should have known the opposite to be true.[1] The consequence was the failure to properly govern and regulate the two government-sponsored enterprises, which contributed substantially to the subprime mortgage meltdown that caused much of the economic pain that ensued. To be fair, the lack of truth-telling was endemic to much of Congress, the cabinet, and the White House. And it didn't stop there. Had those at the top of

Bank of America, Lehman Brothers, AIG, Countrywide, and countless other companies, large and small, told the truth to investors, employees, and customers, the history of those years could almost certainly be written with considerably less heartache and devastation.

Partially as a result of these high-profile breaches of trust (along with many others you and I never heard about), there's more than a healthy degree of *mistrust* among workers (not to mention customers and investors) in leaders, at all levels, and in all kinds of organizations—business, government, religious, and educational institutions.

Trust in those around us acts as a powerful lubricant. It accelerates our work, thoughts, and processes, and the absence of it puts a measurable drag on all that we do. People simply can't execute with speed and precision when they're operating under an excess of dubious assumptions. The contrast between working in an environment of trust and its opposite is analogous to that of driving on a reasonably straight highway on a clear, dry day versus doing so on a serpentine mountain road on a foggy night.

A 2009 poll that worldwide research firm YouGov conducted in the United Kingdom reports that only 15 percent of respondents felt that their employer had communicated news about job security "very well," while 37 percent said communication had been "poor" or "nonexistent." In the same poll, less than half (48 percent) of respondents said they had a clear picture of their company's performance, and only 28 percent said that they trusted messages from their chief executive more than "a little."[2]

And as PepsiCo chief executive officer Indra Nooyi wisely stated, when there's a crisis of trust, people "may not differentiate between guilty and innocent parties—everyone in corporate America could take a share of the blame, deserved or not."[3]

The truth of Nooyi's observation means that the people and organizations we lead could probably benefit from an extra measure of vigilance on our part, with respect to telling the truth. We simply can't expect people to be candid with us and tell us what we as leaders need to know if they can't rely on us to tell them the truth—good or bad.

A lie gets halfway around the world before the truth has a chance to get its pants on.

—Winston Churchill

Although the preceding quote gives us a good chuckle, we think that had Mr. Churchill lived in the Internet age, he might have reversed the positions of "a lie" and "the truth" and said even more of a mouthful. Think about it; there's simply no way to hide the truth these days. Never mind the "news" media, any reasonably functional 15-year-old with an iPhone and Google can get at information—true or not—in less than 5 minutes! Before you've had a chance to craft a "reasonable explanation," your audience has already formulated an opinion. No greater argument exists to compel leaders to get out in front and speak the truth.

During a self-imposed out-of-town blackout to maximize task focus while writing this book, my brother had a surprise hospital visit as a result of something that had the potential to be serious. My family hesitated to let me know, not wanting to break my concentration. Figuring, however, that I'd probably learn eventually, via one electronic portal or another, they went ahead and called. There is little doubt that, just as in the work-place, it might have been easier for them to conveniently remain silent and let me find out later. I was glad they decided that I could handle the truth. Your employees can, too.

Truth isn't always beauty, but the hunger for it is.

—Nadine Gordimer

The Strength of Coffee, Steel, and the Truth

Telling the truth often requires courage—the kind of courage plucked up by Starbucks CEO and *Fortune*'s 2011 Businessperson of the Year, Howard Schultz, when he took on the role of political activist. In September 2011, Schultz publicly declared his disgust at the dysfunction of the government in Washington, DC, pledged to withhold political action committee (PAC) money from incumbents of both political parties, and encouraged other CEOs to do the same. A few weeks later, he announced in full-page ads in both the *New York Times* and *USA Today* that more than 140 other CEOs had joined him in his crusade. Since political con-tributions are the currency with which legislative influence is bought, Schultz's speaking truth to power displayed considerable and respectable backbone.

Other truth-tellers include Nucor (the largest steel manufacturer in the United States) CEO Dan DiMicco, who along with his predecessors has cultivated a habit of keeping faith and being honest with the company's employees. The truth of late hasn't been pretty, as the recession has hit the steel industry in a particularly vicious way. Through it all, however, Nucor has remained transparent to its workers and has protected their jobs. They've never laid off an employee due to a work shortage in their history. Nucor employees have returned the favor by never once voting to unionize in an otherwise highly unionized industry.

Nobody's Perfect

Neither employees, customers, nor other stakeholders expect us to get everything right all the time. Yet people will forgive all kinds of imperfections in their leaders—boneheaded decisions, bad calls, even momentary lapses in humility—before they're willing to grant a pardon for being dishonest. A good old-fashioned apology, coupled with a humble acceptance of responsibility, can turn many failures into opportunities for redemption.

You don't have to be a huge fan of Facebook or its founder Mark Zuckerberg to appreciate his honest response to a misreading of customers' desires a few years after he launched the social networking service.

"We really messed this one up. When we launched News Feed and Mini-Feed we were trying to provide you with a stream of information about your social world. Instead, we did a bad job of explaining what the new features were and an even worse job of giving you control of them. I'd like to try to correct those errors now."[4] Judging from the steady growth of Facebook's wealth, footprint, and influence in the world, we'd say that most customers let go of the grudge.

Liar, Liar

Now, we are not suggesting that the whole world gets up in the morning and says, "I think I'll go to work and tell a fib today." Lying is (usually) not that deliberate or direct, yet it frequently seems second nature in workplace situations, and to be honest, it often starts before the person is even hired.

Most managers walk around with the well-founded suspicion that people are going to lie to them from the start—even during the employment interview. And many do, to be sure. But how often do they receive the same in kind before the interview is even halfway through? Consider whether the following exchange sounds familiar:

Applicant: So what's it like working around here?

Manager: *[preoccupied with getting the wash out, the project managed, burgers flipped, etc.]* It's a great place to work . . . almost like family. *[Yeah, the dysfunctional sort.]*

Applicant: How will I learn the job?

Manager: Oh, we've got an extensive onboarding and training program. *[Right—one that probably lasts all morning.]*

Applicant: What are the big bosses like?

Manager: They're great people. They really believe in putting others first. Just look here in our annual report at what our chairman and CEO said: "I am confident because I am so proud of the job being done by our more than 300,000 people." *[Was that before or after all the layoffs, buyout offers, and your obscene bonus?]*

The principle of "truth or consequences" is certainly simple enough. Yet companies violate it regularly as they spew forth one philosophy while practicing quite another. We're merely suggesting that PR should take a distant backseat to honesty—especially when it comes to communicating with your workforce. If your company is a tough place to work, say so, and be very explicit in explaining why and how. And don't apologize for it! If your business is in trouble, say so. And for Pete's sake, if an employee is screwing up, tell them. That's what managers get paid for. Either step up to the plate or go sit in the dugout!

Seeking to avoid the shackles that unionism and our judicial system have imposed over the past decades, American industry—largely at the urging of HR practitioners and labor attorneys—has adopted an overly conservative (some might call it mealy mouthed) approach to dealing with employee performance issues. The atmosphere of caution is so pervasive that while tiptoeing around possible charges of discrimination, favoritism, wrongful discharge, and the like, managers have often completely lost sight of the mission at hand—namely, fixing performance errors! And yet we wonder why it's so difficult to improve things like quality and productivity and why people get so upset with us when we finally *do* tell them there's a problem with their performance.

Malice in Wonderland

We did some work for a company whose identity we'll protect by calling it Giant. With nearly $2 billion in annual revenues and an employee population near 40,000, the company was sizable indeed. However, because they terminated the services of a high number of employees for performance-related reasons, Giant's management determined that they had a problem. For example, they fired some 986 people in one 18-month span—not due to egregious transgressions such as lying, cheating, or stealing, but simply for doing a crummy job. Tasked by the CEO with looking into this and coming up with some answers, we began investigating the situation. We searched in all the usual places and talked to all the usual suspects—some of the "firees" as well as the managers who had done the dastardly deeds. We combed through HR records, examined hiring practices, and did a robust search through Giant's rather sophisticated HR information system.

At some point, we learned of "Giant's Performance Review Policy," which was pretty standard: it required formal written reviews every six months until death or termination. A staff member sifted through the HR system, trying to find a correlation between poor reviews and the terminations, but quickly returned with the news that there was "obviously a flaw in either the data itself or the search parameters, as no correlation could be found." Wait a minute! Upon further review the conclusion was the same: no correlation between the reviews and the terminations. Giant managers had dutifully conducted performance reviews with every one of these 986 people in the six months immediately preceding their termination. However, they had *informed* the employee that they were doing an unsatisfactory job in only three of those cases. Roughly two-thirds of these same people had also received merit increases in the six months preceding their termination. As sad is it is, what was happening at Giant is more the rule than the exception. In fact, it's probably going on right now in your company. Go find out!

Not Every Performance Deserves a Standing Ovation

As a big fan of musical theater and the parent of an aspiring performer, I've been to lots of shows. In my experience, most performances in the United States (unless embarrassingly lousy) receive a standing ovation, deserved or not. Once in a while, after a truly remarkable performance, the standing O is spontaneous, immediate, and unanimous. More often, it starts with a few enthusiastic supporters, then those who think, "Yeah, that was pretty good. I guess I'll stand like these other people," and finally a more reluctant group who stand so they don't look like soreheads.

On a recent visit to the United Kingdom, my wife and I attended a well-done performance of Rodgers and Hammerstein's *Oklahoma!* At the end of the show, the audience showed its intense appreciation with thunderous and sustained applause—from a seated position. The cast took their bows. The audience kept clapping and whistling . . . and sitting. It was altogether appropriate feedback for the performance. Although worthy of such applause, it was *not* among the *very* best I, or apparently the rest of the audience, had ever seen. Don't get me wrong. On a scale of 1 to 5, it was a solid 4. But standing ovations, like the top rating on a performance evaluation, should be reserved for those performances that are truly distinguished in their excellence. We're not telling the truth when we give everybody a "5," "Outstanding," or "Consistently Exceeds Expectations"—and as a result, it cheapens the feedback that an evaluation is meant to impart. I imagine that the *Oklahoma!* cast left the stage that night thinking something like, "We did well, and we can improve even beyond that. And maybe we'll bring them to their feet if we do."

We're all for positive feedback. However, we're even more in favor of accurate, helpful feedback. You want your employees to know you as a straight shooter. Tell someone when he or she has room for improvement, and then help them get the rest of the way. We're doing no favors when we tell people they've reached the summit, when the summit is actually still just a few yards away. Reserve the standing ovations for those performances that are truly in a singular place at the top. And don't be afraid to stand and clap when you find them.

The trouble with most of us is that we would rather be ruined by praise than saved by criticism.

—Norman Vincent Peale

To Tell the Truth

Before we leave the subject of truth-telling, we'd like to offer some practical help on ways to make it, if not easier, perhaps a little less painful to tell people what they deserve to hear when the news isn't packed with fun.

1. In general, tell them *sooner rather than later*. There are a few, but only a few, good reasons to wait:

   a. You need to get more facts yourself.

   b. Someone else needs to know first.

   c. The time or place is not conducive to hearing what you've got to tell them.

2. If you're responsible for the problem, own it, and say so. When we hear the words, ". . . apologized, but admitted no wrongdoing," it's a safe bet that lawyers are running the show.

3. If you're *not* responsible, be clear about that too. However, worry less about fingering the suspect and more about doing whatever's in your realm to put the situation on a more positive course, if possible.

4. Be scrupulously honest when it comes to performance feedback, but put away the battering ram. Don't cloud the message with weasely language that you hope will soften the blow. Instead, offer ways to improve along with your help and support as they take responsibility to do so.

5. Finally, make it easier for others to tell *you* the truth. Don't shoot the messengers. In fact, thank them. Reward them. Create mechanisms that naturally result in more good information coming your way.

I didn't lie to anyone.

—Don Shula, when asked what he'd like to be remembered for

Chapter Summary

1. If you care about your people, you tell them the truth—period.

2. People need to hear bad news directly from the person who made the decision, rather than read it in a report, in an e-mail, on Facebook, or in a tweet. And they deserve to hear it as early as possible.

3. The greatest problem with performance reviews is not the form, the frequency, or the lack of objectivity, but a lack of honesty!

4. Just like at home where we teach our children to lie at an early age ("Tell 'em Daddy's not here" when the phone rings), we begin early at work—often before people are even on our payroll!

5. Not every performance deserves a standing ovation. Save the standing and clapping for those that do.

Worst Practice:

1. "Giant's" performance review policy (and probably yours).

CHAPTER

7

When Times Get Tough

If you take care of your employees, they'll take care of your customers and the customers will keep coming back.
— J. Willard Marriott Sr., founder, Marriott International

If You Care, You're There

Perhaps more than anything else they can do, organizations and their leaders can demonstrate that they care by their willingness to go the extra mile when times get tough. Very often, that demonstration occurs simply by being physically present when their workers, customers, or communities are experiencing difficulty.

In our view, there *is* something of a quid pro quo involved here. Recall from the first chapter that *discretionary effort* is, by definition, a contribution people can make if—but only if—they want to. The conscious decision to part with some of that discretionary effort is based, at least in part, on the individual's perception of how things would go if the shoe were on the other foot. In other words, "You're asking me to walk through fire for you? Would you—or *have you*—done the same for me?"

One of the reasons that Marriott International is able to capture so much of their staff members' "spirit to serve" is that they have demonstrated time and again that the company will pull out all the stops in times of need.

Marriott's Response to Hurricane Katrina: Quick, Compelling, Sustained

When Hurricane Katrina struck the central Gulf Coast region and unleashed its fury on August 29, 2005, more than 1,800 people lost their lives and many thousands more were cast into misery. This most debilitating and paralyzing natural disaster in U.S. history caused an estimated $81 billion in damage and, according to estimates from the U.S. Department of Labor, cost the short-term loss of more than 230,000 jobs.[1] Although valuable help poured in from countless national and global organizations, few responded with more compassion and practical help than Marriott.

With 21 properties in Louisiana, Alabama, and Mississippi closed by the storm, and more than 2,800 employees impacted, Marriott mobilized quickly to meet its people's—and their communities'—short-term and continuing needs. They worked vigorously to restore area operations and their employees' jobs. Just a few days after the storm clouds cleared, the company established the Marriott and Ritz-Carlton Disaster Relief Fund to care for affected Marriott associates' immediate and longer-term needs.

Many of the company's property owners, guests, and suppliers joined the Marriott family in building the fund, which eventually raised $5.6 million for Katrina victims and remains in place today to benefit those touched by future disasters. Marriott associates from around the world supported fellow workers by donating vacation time and cash to the relief fund.

To their credit, Marriott management realized that there was no time for a committee to study "best practices" or to worry about what was procedurally correct with respect to providing help. Within days of Katrina's landfall, each affected associate received a $500 check to help meet their immediate needs. As many had no habitable place to stay, associates and their families were moved into Marriott hotels and fed in their restaurants. Everyone continued to receive their pay and benefits through the month of September, and the donated vacation time was converted to cash and used to further extend associate benefits coverage from October to December. Suspending its rules designed for ordinary times, the company also provided immediate cash payouts for all qualifying associates with accrued paid time off balances.

Once the company had fed and sheltered employees and their families, they focused on providing longer-term housing assistance. More than $3 million was distributed to 1,749 associates to help pay for rent, mortgages, and home repair expenses.

The rehabilitation and recovery of New Orleans was to be a long and difficult process, punctuated by periods both of success and of frustration. Marriott decided to further invest in the community by partnering with Habitat for Humanity International to build homes throughout New Orleans, and then with KaBOOM! to build playgrounds in particularly hard-hit areas where many of the company's associates lived.

Although Marriott management acted the way they did because it was the right thing to do, there can be little doubt that it will be a long time before their 150,000 worldwide employees forget how the company treated some of their own in a time of need.

> *When a team member is enduring a personal hardship, we want you to go above and beyond for that person. When you do, you will have their full attention when you talk about going above and beyond for our customers.*
> —Dan Cathy, President and chief operating officer, Chick-fil-A, addressing a group of new store operators and managers

Hanmer MSL's Response to the Mumbai Bombings

The evening rush hour in Mumbai, India, on July 13, 2011, was shattered by a terrorist act that included three successive bomb blasts that claimed an estimated 27 lives and left more than 130 injured. The city's initial shock and paralysis quickly gave way to frenetic action by those trying to calm the area's 20 million inhabitants—including about 300 employees of Hanmer MSL, a major public relations and social media marketing company headquartered in the subcontinent's largest metropolis. The company that had built a name, in part, on helping organizations communicate in times of crisis was now eating its own cooking.

Chief executive officer Jaideep Shergill and senior manager Prashanti Mikayla told us that their top priorities were to first protect their employees' safety and then to quickly communicate clear, accurate information to all of their workers and their families, in Mumbai and elsewhere. "There was so much confusion in the initial hours," Mikayla told us. "Nobody knew who was responsible for the bombings or where the next blast might occur." A number of the company's managers and employees were in the office when the blasts occurred toward the end of the workday; however, others were scattered among various parts of the city, on their way home, or with clients. "The first thing that we, as the leadership team, communicated among ourselves was that everyone who could, needed to come to the office to 'be physically present' where the employees could see and talk to us," Mikayla told us. "Next, it was important to be able to source the most dependable information about the on-ground reality so that [we could take] the right course of action on behalf of the employees and the organization. Being in the media and communications industry worked well for us, as we were able to effectively leverage the network we'd built over the years."

After efforts to account for every employee (eventually, all were found safe), Hanmer's leaders urgently wanted to give employees' families assurance that their loved ones were okay. However, central Mumbai's jammed phone lines posed a major obstacle. Mikayla shared with us the following account:

> The [jammed] telephone lines made communication extremely difficult. But the phones outside the city and in other locations where we have offices were working fine. Our employees wanted to tell their families—who were of course extremely worried—that they were okay. [Their relatives] kept seeing all of this on the news, but no one could get in touch, so many could only assume the worst. So we turned to e-mail and social media platforms such as Facebook and Twitter to communicate with our employees in other cities, who in turn called our Mumbai employees' families. This worked remarkably well!

The emphasis on leaders being there, in person, and the urgency and sensitivity with which they handled the communication of reassurance sent an unmistakable message to Hanmer MSL's employees that they worked for a company that cares—and one that demonstrates that caring, especially in times of crisis. In Mikayla's words, "I feel that great workplaces are painstakingly created through trust and engagement between organizations and their employees, and that results in greater loyalty and retention."

Caring Means Going the Extra Mile

Mitchel MacNair joined the U.S. Navy straight out of high school and married his childhood sweetheart after his first year of service. The day after the wedding, the Navy packed and moved the MacNairs' belongings (unopened wedding gifts and all) to MacNair's next duty station in upstate New York. Shortly after the newlyweds arrived in their new home, they were notified that the moving van with all their worldly goods had been broken into and that everything had been stolen. Tough way to start a marriage. As if that weren't enough, the Navy's processes at the time meant that the couple had to wait six months before being reimbursed for the monetary value of their loss.

Fast-forward to 1998, when MacNair was hired by the Dow Chemical Company in Houston for his first post-Navy job as an instrumentation engineer. Their first child was only a few months old when the MacNairs arrived in Houston. The Navy had placed all of their belongings in storage in San Antonio until they were able to find a permanent residence. Again, the Navy bureaucracy ground slowly and MacNair learned that it would take three weeks for his stuff to make the 200-mile trip from San Antonio to Houston.

When MacNair's boss learned that his new employee's family was going to have to sleep on the floor and stand up a lot for a few weeks, he decided to intervene. The manager immediately called a furniture rental company and arranged to have everything the MacNairs needed delivered to their home the next day. MacNair told us, "When I say everything, I mean EVERYTHING," including plants and pictures of people the MacNairs didn't even know, to hang on the walls.

MacNair and his wife were completely overwhelmed, and both instantly became, as he put it, "The number one fans of Dow Chemical." "I've been with Dow for over 13 years now," MacNair says, "and I would never think of leaving. Dow has just been too good to my family and me, and that experience with my first boss left an indelible impression on us."

So indelible an impression, in fact, that MacNair has told the story to lots of people over the years, and he eagerly shares it when recruiting highly sought after candidates for Dow.

Employee Engagement in a Headwind

Workers, jobs, and economic output weren't the only victims of the 2007–2009 great recession. Employee engagement fared poorly too. Workers felt squeezed by organizations struggling to survive, and leaders too often failed to realize that the only way to survive a tough economy is by attaining every employee's full, willing engagement.

A 2009 study by nonprofit business research group the Conference Board reported that only 45 percent of workers surveyed claimed to be satisfied in their jobs, down from 61 percent in 1987.[2] Unlike the economy, this downward trend has been constant, not cyclical. Just like gravity, job satisfaction has gone but one way of late: down.

Global consulting firm Mercer conducted a 2011 study whose report carried the headline "Post Recession Environment Yields Increasingly Disengaged Workforce." The study reported that 32 percent of employees polled were "seriously considering leaving" their jobs, up from 23 percent in 2005. An additional 21 percent said they had a negative view of their employer and had largely checked out of their job, even if they weren't looking for another one.[3] Simple math yields the discomforting revelation that, based on this study, more than half the workforce has unplugged and taken their game home, while still taking up space, precious oxygen . . . and a paycheck. British consultancy Reabur.com reported in the same year that 31 percent of U.K. workers were "unhappy" in their jobs, and 7 percent went so far as to say they "hated" them.[4]

Westport, Connecticut–based psychologist Hendrie Weisinger offers the following list of what gets the American worker hot under the proverbial collar, be it of the white or blue variety. We suspect that these items (listed in no particular order) needn't be confined to the American workforce:

1. Harassment, sexual or otherwise
2. Favoritism of one employee over another

3. Insensitivity of managers

4. Depersonalization of the workplace, causing employees to feel as if they're just numbers

5. Unfair performance appraisals

6. Lack of resources, including everything from support staff to corporate credit cards

7. Lack of adequate training

8. Lack of teamwork

9. Withdrawal of earned benefits

10. Lack or violation of trust

11. Poor communication

12. Absentee bosses

Although aggrieved employees may appear to do nothing about the situation on the surface, the fact remains that people really don't forget about their perceived injustices. Rather, they file them away and accumulate others until they reach a breaking point—at which time they escalate their demand for justice.

All too often, an employee who has moved on to a more overt plan of action will find someone else to help them with the problem. Although the number of people turning to unions to accomplish this has steadily declined over the past 30 years, we can't count organized labor out.

A 2011 attempt by Wisconsin's newly inaugurated governor Scott Walker to sharply curtail the collective bargaining rights of most of the state's public sector unions drew thousands of protesters to the capitol in Madison for weeks. The fury over this issue, along with other state employee concessions and budget actions, was not about to go away. Eleven months later, 1 million Wisconsinites (nearly one-third of the state's registered voters) signed petitions in favor of a recall election to "deselect" the governor.

It should be clear by now that we're not big fans of unions. In fact, much of our work over the past 30 years has focused on helping organizations obviate unions by maintaining a positive employee relations culture in which both the individual and the organization can do their best work and gain the most from it. That said, we respect every worker's right to make a choice as to whether or not they are willing to enter into a direct, cooperative, mutually beneficial relationship with their management. That choice is most often based on whether or not management has earned the benefit of the doubt. If the answer is yes, workers feel no need to reach out and seek (let alone pay for) the protection of organized labor.

Meanwhile, it has become increasingly popular for people to involve other outside advocates such as agents, lawyers, or state or federal agencies to get what they want. According to the American Bar Association, there were more than 1.2 million "resident and active" lawyers in the United States in 2010 (32,000 of them on federal payrolls alone). That's one lawyer for every 260 persons. And if statistics released by the U.S. Equal Employment Opportunity Commission are any indication, all those attorneys have been working overtime; the years 2008 through 2010 saw a period of sharp and steady increases in the number of suits filed for unlawful discrimination and harassment, with the figure in 2010 being the highest in the agency's 45-year history.

> *Stay away from the courthouse; you'll never make any money there.*
> —J.E. Davis, founder, Winn-Dixie Stores

Give Us Some Recourse

Contented Cow organizations realize that whenever you've got two or more people working in some common endeavor, perceived injustices and serious problems will arise from time to time. They realize too that most people really don't *want* to sue their employer, join a labor union, or involve an outside agency, let alone quit their job. So rather than waiting to be victimized by one or another of the self-prescribed remedies, these companies proactively install a system that tolerates and even encourages the airing and resolution of the problem so that people can get on with the business at hand.

Atlanta-area human resources pro Kim Scholes, who now works in the private sector, gained the bulk of her experience in alternative dispute resolution (ADR) while she was with a heavily unionized department of the federal government. As Scholes explains, "We used a 'Win-Win

Bargaining' model an as alternative to the more formal union grievance procedure every time it was appropriate. Not only did most employees like it better, but it gave everyone a much faster way to get things resolved. We found that, before very long, the number of grievances and even Unfair Labor Practice filings went way down."

Mike Field is the employee and labor relations manager for Dopaco, a Philadelphia-area company that manufactures packaging for quick-service restaurants, through a network of six plants, three of which have union representation and three that do not. Several years ago, while one of the company's nonunion plants was in the midst of a union-organizing campaign, Field was speaking with a worker who was supporting the union's potential involvement at the plant.

"You know what the problem is here, Mike," the worker said. "We have no recourse. When you guys want to discipline somebody, we have nowhere to turn, and that's why I think we need the union."

This man's comment put the wheels in motion. It wasn't so much the union that the workers wanted, but a system of justice and some means of recourse. Soon after a majority of the plant's workers voted *not* to seek union representation, he assembled a team comprised of members of both rank-and-file and management to research, develop, and implement what was to become a highly successful peer review process known as EAAAS (Employee Adverse Action Appeal System).

Dopaco's process was designed principally to adjudicate disciplinary action vis-à-vis the company's policies and procedures. According to Field, "This was one of the most rewarding activities I've ever been involved in, because it [allowed] management and the employees [to work] together on a project that was aimed at helping everyone."

Apparently the process is working. Not only did the atmosphere in the plant improve after EAAAS, because, in Field's view, "the employees felt we'd listened to them and provided a fair means of recourse to them," but there was never any more union-organizing activity in the facility. And there were significant side benefits as well. Because the process involved renewed training of managers on the company's disciplinary policies, there were far fewer incidents in which an employee felt the need to question the actions that were taken. And because managers would naturally rather avoid the process in the first place, they've taken a proactive stand to do a better job when correcting performance and behavior issues. And finally, EAAAS lets employees know that their managers have given due consideration to disciplinary issues before actions are taken.

"One really good piece of advice we got," Field told us, "[which is advice] I'd give to anyone considering something like this: you can't make this a cookie-cutter plan. You've got to customize it to fit your specific set of circumstances."

Whether you decide to implement something like Dopaco's peer review process or some other form of alternative dispute resolution in your organization, keep in mind that people will always seek an advocate or "some recourse," as the Dopaco worker put it. As leaders, *we* can help design that recourse, or let others do it for themselves. It's our call.

Don't Expect Employees to Pay for Your Mistakes

Another way that companies demonstrate whether or not they care is how much they expect people to pay for managers' mistakes. Sometimes employees are asked to give up perks they once enjoyed, and this isn't always a bad thing to do, especially in light of the alternatives. But people take an understandably dim view of the matter when that sacrifice is caused by (or occurs in the face of) managerial indiscretions or extravagances.

Consider, for example, the case of a large southern hospital. When faced with the prospect of having to lay off more than 100 full-time employees, they decided instead on an ambitious cost-cutting program, which is detailed in the following excerpt from a message conveyed to all hospital staff (our editorial comments appear in brackets):

MEMO

As part of our Continuous Quality Improvement process [please!], we must continually look for ways to improve efficiency. This is particularly true in today's environment with respect to reimbursement. One way to do that is to reduce expenses, which places us in a better position to bid on health care contracts. [It sounds rational . . . so far.]

As we receive more contracts because of lower cost pricing, the probability of future stable employment will increase. [Yeah, right. We'll have to wait and see about that.]

Effective [such-and-such date], the following "expense improvements" [write that one down] will be implemented:

- Hourly shifts will be cut from 13 to 12 hours and overtime will be eliminated, saving $1.2 million.

- The 5 holidays for which we now pay premium overtime will be reduced to 3, saving $127,000.

- The weekend differential will be cut from 30 percent to $2/hour, saving $806,000.

- The number of Compensated Days Off for salaried employees will be cut from 13 to 8, saving $227,000.

- The tuition reimbursement plan will be eliminated, saving $1.2 million. [In other words, we're convinced that having less educated employees will help our bottom line].

- The total cost savings of the above will total more than $3.5 million, allowing us to stabilize employment for 107 full-time employees.

On the surface, the message doesn't sound too unreasonable. It's kind of the old "let's all pull together to keep this boat afloat" idea, one which we support. Yet it mysteriously left out information about the $4.1 million capital expenditure in the same year for such health-improving hospital features as a new marble entranceway, expanded lobby complete with a $1 million aquarium and attendant staff, and new china for executive functions.

The grumbling over the cost cuts turned to loud shouts and defections when the opulence was installed. And a year after all the selective belt tightening, a hundred more people received "unstable employment"; in other words, they were laid off. All we can say is that we're glad neither of us lives close enough to this hospital to actually have to depend on it for health care. We imagine there are some pretty Discontented Cows running around the place. And although we're sure they're all behaving professionally, we don't even want to think about the dangerous combination of a Mad Cow with a needle or proctoscope!

While the eventual layoffs at the hospital may seem cruelly handled and only halfheartedly forestalled, "guaranteed employment" is every bit as unjust and unkind—especially in the economic environment in which we've been living for the past few years.

Sometimes a change of pasture will make the cow fatter.

—American frontier saying

Layoffs—A Fact of Life

The great recession saw a predictable resurgence in layoff activity all over the United States and abroad. The more than doubling of the U. S. unemployment rate, from 4.6 percent in 2007 to 9.6 percent in 2010, rested largely on the backs of workers who received the dreaded message, "You don't get to work here anymore. It's not because of anything you did, but because we can't afford to keep paying you." The better leaders in the better-run companies delivered these messages in person. Others took the cowardly way out and shared the news by phone, letter, or e-mail. Real class. And although some of the downsizing was unavoidable, much was not.

Although there's little evidence that layoffs lead to better performing organizations in the long run, some layoff decisions in the past few years were a matter of survival. In other cases, bloated organizations took advantage of the economic timing to shed some affordable, if not altogether indispensable, weight.

Fueled by general conjecture that society was somewhat more forgiving of tough decisions in periods of economic turmoil, a kind of "everybody else is doing it" mentality took over. This allowed many organizations to feel as though they could downsize without suffering much damage to their corporate reputations. Only time will tell how safe a bet that turns out to be.

Organization development researchers McKinley, Schick, and Sanchez point out that "while downsizing has been viewed primarily as a cost reduction strategy, there is considerable evidence that downsizing does not reduce expenses as much as desired, and that sometimes expenses may actually increase."[5]

Although most organizations have a pretty clear picture of the payroll savings they can expect from sending large groups of people home, most substantially underestimate the following cost of such actions—which can wipe out the gains promised by the restructuring:

1. Severance cost and increase in unemployment insurance premium.

2. Damage to employer brand (the hoped-for "everybody's doing it" immunity is probably more illusion than reality).

3. Cost of impaired morale and decreased engagement. (For example— if a 500-person firm loses the goodwill and the discretionary effort of 475 survivors when they ham-handedly whack 25 heads, is it really worth it?)

4. Gutting of the leadership pipeline. Think about it. When you lay off large groups of employees, you greatly increase the chance that you're firing a future company leader. You won't know who it is, but the effect is still real. Executives in companies that executed severe cutbacks in the 1980s reported a heavy price that had to be paid 20 years later when they needed experienced, knowledgeable leaders— and found only a broad empty space in the ranks.

There are at least two ways to look at the issue of downsizing. First, as the frequency and pace of change in the commercial landscape increase, companies are propelled in and out of business sectors and markets at an ever more rapid rate. It is undeniable that the days when employees could reasonably expect to have a one-company career if they so wished are pretty much over, perhaps forever. From now on, nearly all businesses will continue to find themselves reacting to an oversupply or undersupply of labor as they relentlessly pursue ways to do things better, faster, and cheaper.

No matter how great the hue and cry is over management's obsession with the short-term outlook, market forces have spoken. In fact, given that nearly everyone these days has money in the market (via a 401(k) or IRA), a Wisconsin schoolteacher is just as inclined as any Wall Street analyst to raise hell when earnings don't meet or exceed targets every quarter. In an interview during an earlier period of downsizing, Peter Lynch, former manager of Fidelity's Magellan Fund, pretty much echoed this thought: "All of us are looking for the best deals in clothing, computers, and telephone service—and rewarding the high-quality, low-cost providers with our business," he observed. "I haven't met one person who would agree to pay AT&T twice the going rate for phone service if AT&T would promise to stop laying people off."[6]

However, it's also necessary to look at things from the opposite side of the fence. It's a given that the extent to which employees are concerned about the prospect of losing their jobs mirrors inversely the extent to which they are likely to be concerned with *doing* their jobs. In short, Worried Cows don't make very productive (let alone, Contented) Cows. The folks you are counting on to deliver high-quality goods or a fantastic experience to your customers shouldn't be so busy worrying about their own futures that they can't *care* about the business.

Our view falls somewhere between these two sides. Although layoffs are indeed necessary at times, there is a big difference between grudgingly accepting them as a final desperate act of corporate survival and engaging in what Springfield Remanufacturing CEO Jack Stack once called corporate insanity—that is, using them as a convenient way to periodically trim a little fat. In either case, however, there's no getting around the fact that they are a sign of management failure. According to Stack, "You lay people off when you've screwed up, when you've guessed wrong about the market, [or] when you haven't anticipated some critical development or created adequate contingency plans. It's a sign of how badly management has failed, and the people who get hurt are invariably those who had nothing to do with creating the problem in the first place."[7]

Some Rules for "Staying Out of the Soup"

Here are some precepts that we believe will help you avoid this unpleasantness altogether, if you'll only execute them faithfully:

1. Worry 10 times as much about the quality of employees you add to your payroll as the number of them. As Machiavelli said, "The first method for estimating the intelligence of a ruler is to look at the men he has around him."

2. Adopt outrageously high performance expectations, continually raise the bar, and regularly reassign or remove people who don't

measure up. And don't allow loyalty to be confused with competence as you're executing these processes. Do it humanely; but *do it*. Initiate a career change for managers who can't or won't do this.

3. Eliminate every single systemic inducement to adding unnecessary head count. Never, for example, tie anyone's pay or perks to the number of people they supervise.

4. After doing items 1 to 3, be as judicious about adding head count at work as you are at home.

5. Finally, don't allow profitability or "affordability" to cloud your judgment or lower your standards on any of the above—ever.

The way in which your workforce (and the buying public) perceives layoffs comes down, in the end, to your corporate mind-set. If your organization considers it acceptable to hire people full-time one day and then send them home a few months or years later—simply because you've miscalculated your requirement for labor or ability to profitably sell a product or service—then it's clear to everyone that you *don't* care.

Some organizations are characterized by a sort of binge-and-purge personality—corporate bulimics, if you will. They're caught up in a capricious cycle of staffing up and laying off to meet labor demands exactly. We are not talking about hiring temps or making a strategic decision to permanently outsource certain noncore activities. Rather, we mean those companies that routinely hire and fire because they erroneously think it's a good way to do business. Rarely, if ever, do they acknowledge the consequences of the emotional upheaval visited upon the employees involved—not only those who leave, but particularly the ones who stay—and its concomitant impact on the overall health of the organization.

We know that most CEOs agonize a great deal over the decision to send some people home in order to preserve others' jobs. They must conclude at times—thoughtfully and regretfully—that this is the only (albeit unfortunate) course of action to take. If you *do* find yourself in the unenviable position of having to send people home, there are some things you can do to make it easier on all concerned:

1. Make sure that you've first exhausted all alternative remedies (shortened workweeks, voluntary pay reductions, job reassignments, and

the like). Bring some of the functions you've outsourced back in house and let your own people do the work. People who have demonstrated themselves as nonperformers should be dealt with as such, in advance of any workforce reduction.

2. Get it over with quickly and at once. Sudden death is bad enough, but the lingering variety is unconscionable.

3. Make sure that the pain inflicted on top management occurs first and is clearly disproportionate. Officers must bleed first, and most. Get rid of the corporate toys, squeeze the corporate headquarters, and shrink high-priced management.

4. Don't hide anything from anybody. Your rationale for making these moves needs to be painfully evident and unassailable. Failure to make this case will fuel understandable anger and frustration, not to mention a permanent loss of trust.

5. When it's over, say so and mean it. Turn your attention immediately to enacting serious measures that will help you make damn sure you don't have to go down this road again.

There's Got to Be Another Way!

And as it turns out, there *are* other ways, besides mass layoffs, to stay afloat when labor supply rises above demand. One of our favorite examples comes from Charlotte, North Carolina–based steel manufacturer Nucor, a company with more than 50 U.S. facilities. Despite having come off some of the worst years in its history, including a loss of $294 million in 2009, Nucor is famous for never having laid anyone off. "It's not a policy; it's a practice," says Jerry Richie, a production manager at the company's plant in Oak Creek, Wisconsin.

Nucor's ability to (so far) operate without a layoff stems from its unique culture, coupled with a compensation structure that emphasizes pay for performance at all levels, from the manufacturing floor to the executive offices. The "deal," which all workers understand before day 1, is that their pay will be high when production demand is; when it's down, compensation follows suit. The recent downturn in business hasn't been easy on Nucor's workers, but they've kept their jobs as well as their faith in a management that held up their end of the bargain.

"People were severely impacted from a pay standpoint, in terms of hours being cut and our unique bonus structure. But everyone also understood that they kept their jobs and their benefits," Richie said. And those who were at the plant in 2007 haven't forgotten the $8,000 profit sharing check they'd received when times were better.

Nucor workers weren't sitting around twiddling their thumbs. When they weren't making steel, they attended training, did landscaping, and maintained buildings.

Darrell Sabin, CEO of hosemaker Fluid Connector Products of Portland, Oregon, was searching actively for ways to avoid laying people off when he learned of his state's Work Share program. Designed during the 1980s recession and revitalized in response to the latest downturn, the plan allows employers like Sabin to cut worker hours and makes up part of the loss through unemployment insurance. In other words, your employer doesn't have to terminate you, and the state doesn't wind up paying the entire unemployment bill.

Lots of companies cut wages rather than staff, but FedEx did this a bit differently by starting at the top. Executives took a 10 percent cut, with 5 percent for everyone else. FedEx also announced in 2009 that for the first time, it wouldn't be advertising on that year's Super Bowl telecast—another very public effort to save money.

And while shortening the workweek isn't a terribly novel idea, it works. Investment firm Schwab went from Casual Fridays to no Fridays at all, cutting pay by 20 percent but giving everyone a long weekend. And Reading, Pennsylvania–based custom plastic packaging maker Tray-Pak has instituted a four-day workweek during the typically slow months from February until April for the past two years. Most Tray-Pak workers preferred getting paid 80 percent and keeping their benefits to the alternative. It also paid off for the company, which didn't have to reinvest in the costly training program for its manufacturing workers.

When networking giant Cisco saw its fortunes plummet after the tech bubble burst around 2001, it instituted an unusual program called Cisco Community Fellows. Eighty Cisco employees opted to work for nonprofits for a year, pulling down a third of their usual wages rather than cutting ties with the company. During that time, they received employee benefits, vesting, and access to training and continuing education. If jobs opened up, the fellows enjoyed an advantage over external candidates.

Doing Well by Doing Good

One of the best ways to get people's minds off their own situations and provide a little perspective is through a concerted show of support for others less fortunate. And there are plenty of them out there.

Although Hurricane Katrina destroyed many things, it helped strengthen the bonds between Marriott and the international organization Habitat for Humanity, which partners with citizens and organizations to build low-cost homes for new homeowners. Between 2007 and 2010, Marriott associates and managers in the hard-hit Gulf region contributed more than 7,000 labor hours toward building Habitat homes, including six homes for their fellow Marriott workers. One Habitat homeowner, Geraldine Taylor, a housekeeping supervisor at the Ritz-Carlton, New Orleans (a Marriott property), was so appreciative of all that the company had done for her and her son that she now volunteers in the ongoing Marriott Habitat projects.

Working with these kinds of organizations not only is great for the community and aids recipients but can create a powerful team-building opportunity for your employees. I once accompanied my wife to our local Ronald McDonald House when her team had volunteered to feed that night's residents—families of children undergoing treatment for serious medical conditions in nearby hospitals. All I did was carry the food in, and I still left with a great sense of satisfaction from the appreciation of the families who were there.

Publix Super Markets has been a champion for "rescued food" in the markets it serves. The Lakeland, Florida–based chain that has more than 1,000 stores in five southeastern states pledges as part of its mission statement to be "intolerant of waste." They try to reconcile the fact that roughly one-quarter of the food produced in the United States is thrown away, with statistics citing the nearly 50 million Americans who live in "food-insecure" households. One initiative is for Publix and its employee-owners to partner with the North Florida nonprofit agency Waste Not Want Not (among others) to distribute tons of food to families in need—food that may be past its "sell by" date but that is still safe and nutritious and would otherwise go into a landfill, uneaten.

We told you in Chapter 4 that one of Toronto's Maple Leaf Sports and Entertainment's corporate value statements is "Leaders in Our

Community." Demonstrating that those words are more than an idle bullet point on a list of values, the company partners with the area's Second Harvest Food Bank by donating all perishable food items following each of the more than 250 events at Air Canada Centre every year. Maple Leaf players had 100 percent participation in the team's 2012 charitable ticket purchase program, which allowed more than 2,300 kids and nearly 150 military troops to attend a Leafs game. And each holiday season, the company's employees act as bell ringers for the Salvation Army's famous kettle collection drives. The organization is so committed to helping the community that it has its own *TeamingUp* blog, and each year it awards a cash prize of C$3,000 to the employee who has done the most to personify its community leadership value.

Chapter Summary

1. If you care about your people, you're there when times are tough.
2. Everybody needs an advocate.
3. Don't expect your employees to pay for your mistakes.

Better Practices:
1. Marriott's response to Hurricane Katrina
2. Hanmer MSL's response to the Mumbai bombings
3. Dow Chemical's temporary furnishing of the MacNairs' new home
4. Peer review process at Dopaco
5. The Rules for Staying Out of the Soup
6. Nucor's no-layoff practice (not policy)
7. Fluid Connector Product's participation in the Oregon State Work Share plan
8. Publix's rescued food efforts
9. Cisco's Community Fellows

Contented Cows Are Connected

I enjoin you to be ever alert to the pitfalls of too much authority. Beware that you do not fall in the category of the little man with a little job, with a big head. In essence, be considerate, treat your subordinates right, and they will literally die for you.

—Major General Melvin Zais, U.S. Army

Where Everybody Knows Your Name

Pay a visit to the Concierge Lounge in the Marriott Gateway hotel adjacent to Atlanta's Hartsfield-Jackson International Airport, and you will likely meet Joyce Folk, concierge. Each weekday morning, beginning at 6:30, Joyce hosts several dozen of Marriott's most regular guests from all over the world. Many of them stumble in for their morning coffee, breakfast, and maybe a meeting in various states of alertness, dress, and grumpiness. Within seconds of entering the room, Joyce will warmly welcome you.

As a New York native, Joyce's "good morning" doesn't come with the Southern syrup that one might expect in Atlanta, but it's authentic, and that's what counts. And you don't just meet Joyce; she meets you, and gets to know everything about you—your name, where you're from, and as much of your story as you're comfortable relinquishing at that time of day—pretty quickly. And one thing that's certain is that you will never again be a stranger in her lounge. She makes it a point to connect with people, by noticing and then quietly accommodating their habits, preferences, and foibles. One of the more striking observations from spending a few hours in Joyce's company is that nearly everyone in the place knows her by name. In humorous acknowledgment of her role and the high ratio of male guests, she adds, "Yeah, I'm a woman with a hundred husbands."

We do business in Atlanta fairly often, and I can assure you that Joyce and her afternoon counterpart, Crystal, have as much to do with our decision to stay at the Airport Gateway Marriott as do the new facility and its proximity to the airport terminal.

In an age when making someone your Facebook "friend" is too often mistaken for making a true personal connection, Joyce serves as a reminder that decisions to buy from or to follow someone usually have more to do with the relationship than the details of the transaction. And through the other end of the telescope, research suggests that 50 percent of business customers leave not because of a bad product, but a bad experience.

You don't have to talk with Joyce for long to figure out that this 22-year Marriott veteran loves her job and is loyal to her company. And if you knew Joyce, you'd know she wouldn't say it if she didn't believe it. She was recruited from another Atlanta-area Marriott to work at this showcase property even before it opened and told us, "Working for Marriott was my part-time job that I made full-time because of [the company's] loyalty and dedication to the associates." When pressed for specifics on why she felt such a connection to the company, she told us we didn't have enough time for her to tell us everything—"But here's one," she said. "Whenever Mr. Steigerwald comes to Atlanta, he always comes here, and he looks at me and says, 'Hi, Joyce. How are you doing?' He doesn't even look at my name tag. But he knows my name, and he says hello. I think that's cool."

Mr. Steigerwald, by the way, is Rob Steigerwald—Marriott's chief operating officer for Americas, southern region, which includes the southern United States, the Caribbean, and Latin America. This is especially remarkable, given the fact that we've encountered first-level supervisors who couldn't be bothered to learn their employees' names. It's a huge contrast to Rob Steigerwald, and others like him. Leaders at every level who get the best effort from their teams make it a point to invest in their people by getting to know them.

We titled this chapter "Contented Cows Are Connected" to acknowledge the fact that although so many of us today are *over*connected electronically (feel free to tweet anything you read here that you like), most of us have a largely unfulfilled need to be more fully connected—both emotionally and psychologically—to one another, our leaders, our organizations, and the work we do. Contented Cow companies make it a priority to *really, genuinely connect*, with people—usually even before they hire them, and continually throughout the life of the relationship.

During the latter phase of writing this book, we had a chance meeting in Atlanta with a handful of Southwest Airlines leaders, who are managing the Southwest/AirTran integration. When asked what the key to their integration strategy was for merging two very different cultures and operations, we expected to hear something about planes, routes, and fare structures. Instead, we heard two very different things:

1. They gave effusive praise for the pilot and flight attendant workforces who, according to them, had already worked out, without needing to go to arbitration, the always difficult seniority issues that determine everyone's status with the new entity.

2. The senior member of the group piped up and said that *the* single most important part of their strategy was to display, by word and deed to the AirTran workers, that Southwest cares about them.

With an attitude like that, we continue to like their chances, a lot.

Gone are the days when you finish your formal education and immediately begin your career with the organization from which you'll retire decades later. It's no surprise that the U.S. Bureau of Labor Statistics measured average job tenure in the United States at 4.4 years in 2010, down from about 19 years in 1950. Today's workplace derives much more value from the relationship's *strength* than its *length*. Employee engagement today is not so much a question of "How long are you likely to *stay?*" but instead, "How passionately are you likely to contribute while you're here?" We think the answer to that question begins to formulate itself a good while before the first employment document is signed.

Let's Start at the Top—Recruiting

In the same way that consumer brands start making connections with potential buyers before those people ever become customers, Contented Cow employers know that there's no better time to begin capturing their workers' hearts and souls than before those people even *see* an online application.

While millions of unemployed Americans are still competing for too few jobs in countless industries and locations, the so-called Silicon Hills area between Austin and San Antonio is, at least for now, a hotbed of job activity—especially in the tech world. As of this writing, there are simply not enough qualified applicants to fill all of the jobs needed to keep the fire burning along the I-35 corridor of central Texas.

Companies like San Antonio's Rackspace, which calls itself "the service leader in cloud computing," know that you've got to have a lot more than a Careers tab on your website to connect to the talent needed to fuel a growing business. So when you click on their prominent "We Are Hiring!" flag, you end up on a site called rackertalent.com—an entire blog site that's been created to help potential employees get a sense of connection with what *might* be a really cool place to build a career. In reality, you're probably going to bypass the main Rackspace site and go straight to Racker Talent, because someone on Twitter or Facebook, a current employee, or someone who's heard of its employer reputation will have sent you there. Complete with blog posts, videos, and other material from Rackspace employees (called rackers), this portal isn't just a job application website; it's a way for potential rackers to get to know the company before they seriously consider applying. One message, from a racker named Drew, says, "Rackspace doesn't really want you to have a job; they want you to have a life."

Just up the road in Austin we found Ryan Hand, whose title is Recruitment Marketing Guy for a five-year-old company called Bazaarvoice (bazaarvoice.com), a software developer that powers the technology behind online consumer reviews and ratings for such national brands as Best Buy, Sephora, and Procter & Gamble. Check the spelling; it's *bazaar*, as in marketplace. Get it?

Hand's job is to help the company compete for talent—not for customers—with the likes of Rackspace and other tech firms in the region. "We have such a great culture here. I mean we really do, and I'm not just saying that because I'm the Recruitment Marketing Guy. It really is great," he told us, with enthusiasm that would be hard to fake. "It's not like we're doing anything crazy weird here. It's just a great culture to work in."

He portrayed to us the challenge he faces (and loves!) in this highly competitive market for talent as follows: "It's like, I know you work at this amazing place, but come over here and work at this other amazing place." To help make the case, he and his team are continually developing an online portal where prospective employees can get a taste of Bazaarvoice before they ask about signing on. The portal features videos like the one showing the company's annual "Science Fair"—an event where engineers engage in friendly competition for the company's best new ideas. And because people, of course, want to find out a little about their potential colleagues, they'll also find personal profiles for the managers and team leaders. As Hand explains, "This allows us to say, 'Hey, this is who we are, and these are some of the fun people we work with, and this is the cool stuff we're doing. Is this right for you? Is it a good fit?'

"Then when somebody actually comes in, each party is better prepared to have a meaningful conversation. During [the interview], the applicant will say to the interviewing manager, 'Oh, yeah, I saw your video, and I love the research you're doing on JavaScript, and I can't believe you're a huge Frisbee golf fan. So am I.'"

In Hand's view, the most powerful attractions at Bazaarvoice are that "our people get to do what they're passionate about, and the really cool people you get to work with, and I want people to connect with that. I want that to come through, before they even get here. The people we connect with from the beginning—those are the ones who come here and do the best work."

So the trend is set. It's necessary, but insufficient, to only *have* a great culture. Employers who want to find the best talent now open the windows and let potential contributors have a good look around, kick the tires, and make a *connection* before they make a Commitment.

Consolidated Health Services—Ambassadors for Connection

We've long advocated that managers employ something we call re-recruiting, a process whereby companies continue the courtship long after the "knot has been tied" in order to maintain a successful relationship. Indispensable in getting people—especially new hires—Committed to your organization, re-recruiting, or "onboarding on steroids," actually begins at the moment some-one accepts an employment offer. It then continues, realistically, for the life of the employment relationship, with particularly observable bursts of activity in the first year on the job.

We know few employers who do this as well as Consolidated Health Services (CHS). Headquartered in Milford, Ohio, CHS provides home health care services to patients through a network of more than 35 branches throughout Ohio, Indiana, and Kentucky. Talent manager Jennifer Steiger and her boss and vice president of human resources Patty Szelest described to us what happens when a new hire joins the team at this growing company.

CHS has instituted what they call their Ambassador Program in which they pair *every* newly hired associate—whether serving in a clinical or support position—with an experienced employee, or ambassador. This person's job is to welcome the new hire and shepherd him or her through those critical first 120 days in their new position.

Management carefully selects these ambassadors (who must serve will-ingly and by invitation) from among exemplary employees who live the company's mission and values in their work. They wear an identifying pin at work and are recognized at the annual company awards event that names an Ambassador of the Year. This individual is chosen from nomi-nations made by the new employees they helped during the year. Because the ambassador's function is not job specific, he or she may or may not hold the same job as the new employee. Here's how the relationship, and the process, work:

Suppose you've just been hired as, say, a certified nursing assistant (CNA) at CHS, and you're starting your new job in seven days. Your ambassador will call you and begin the conversation with something like this: "We're so excited that you're going to be starting with us next week. I just want to go over a few things to help make that first day an especially good one for you." The ambassador will make sure you know how to get to your office, where to park, and review any traffic considerations. She'll tell you where the drink and snack machines are located and that you'll probably want to bring your lunch most days, but that one of your coworkers is going to take you out to lunch on the first day.

The ambassador will impart information about the time and place for employee orientation and will tell you what to expect in those first few days. She'll likely close her part of the call by saying, "I'll be here at the door to greet you at 8:30 when you arrive, and I'll introduce you to the people you'll be working with. Don't be nervous. Everyone's really looking forward to having you here with us. Do you have any questions for me?"

When the newly hired employee hangs up the phone and picks her jaw up off the floor, she'll probably say to herself, "I have *never* had a call like that from a new employer in my life. I can't wait to get started!"

And when the ambassador hangs up, she'll pick up a note card, specially designed for the Ambassador Program, and pen a handwritten note to the person she just spoke to. Echoing and reviewing some of what was discussed, the card bears a special logo on the front, with the words "Welcome" and "Our team is stronger because of you." On the back are the company's mission, values, "People First" philosophy, and the tagline "We are so happy you are a part of our team!"

And in case the new team member has any doubt as to how welcome they are, they'll find something pretty amazing on their first day: an individualized poster with their name and the same tagline as on the card that was sent. It'll be hanging on the wall of the orientation room and signed by all coworkers, with a message of welcome and encouragement from each one.

It doesn't stop there. The ambassador meets with the new employee weekly during the first two months, and then once a month for the next two months. At the end of 120 days, both ambassador and new(ish) employee have the opportunity to evaluate each other in their respective roles.

> *When employees are happy, they are your very best ambassadors.*
> —Jim Sinegal, chief executive officer, Costco

Connecting in Layers at The Container Store

Without a doubt, the most important and impactful workplace relationship is the one between a worker and his or her immediate supervisor. This connection truly makes all the difference. And when it comes to span of management (that is, the number of people for whom an individual manager has direct leadership responsibility), we've been pretty vocal in our disdain for those workplaces that seem to have a need for one overseer for every six or seven worker bees. Still, at some point, work groups reach a size—depending on individual situations—that breaches leaders' capacity to connect effectively with their members. The inevitable result is a dilution of those crucial relationships. The senior leadership team at The Container Store, the organization and storage retailer that's a perennial entry on top employer rankings, recognized this dilution in their organization—and took action to reverse it.

Conventional wisdom of late has dictated that employers flatten their structure and strip out unnecessary layers of management that don't add value. As raving capitalists, we're all for that. Conventional *practice*, however, has often been to ignore the word *unnecessary* and whack out the layers—whether they add value or not. Yet The Container Store's leadership has bucked this trend and decided to *add* a layer, right in the middle of the chart, at every single store.

In an online interview with Whole Foods Market's Co-CEO John Mackey, The Container Store's CEO Kip Tindell noted that most of their stores formerly had an average of about 80 to 100 employees reporting to a single store manager. Concerned about worker development—and realizing that not even the most talented store manager could adequately address that many employees' needs—Tindell explained that they "added 3, 4, maybe 5 managers to each store. We took the store managers and made them General Manager, and then we added a bunch of management people to nurture, develop, and train, and counsel every person in the store, be they full-time or part-time. It added a lot to store payroll [and] another management layer, the exact opposite of what most people are doing."

Tindell added, "I think it was the best thing we ever did. We already had single-digit turnover. Now that's even lower, the productivity level is higher, and wonderfully enough, payroll—as a percentage of sales—is lower than it was before we added all those people."

Building Affinity at Incepture

Today's workplace is pretty much unrecognizable in many ways from that of even a generation ago. Many of us are no longer chained to a desk, shift, building, department, job, manager, or even an employer, to the degree that was pretty common until fairly recently. As with most significant changes, this disaggregation of work processes and relationships has paid dividends, but not without exacting costs, especially with respect to how connected people feel to their work and employer.

Incepture, the Florida staffing company we introduced in Chapter 5, employs about 50 people at their headquarters to manage more than 700 contractors working in their clients' businesses. The contracting model, which has been a mainstay of the information technology field since long before it caught on elsewhere, works particularly well in project-oriented and certain other situations. However, it presents challenges that contractors, their employers, and the clients must all work together to manage.

Shortly after Earnie Franklin assumed the leadership of Incepture, he began to notice that "our contract professionals didn't have an affinity with us." "They couldn't figure out who they worked for," he said, something he considered to be quite inconsistent with the kind of business he wanted to build. The contract professionals naturally feel connected to the client organizations they serve. However, because they're on Incepture's payroll, they are Incepture employees in every way. As such, Franklin wanted to develop a closer relationship between his contracted employees and the company, without diminishing their value to their clients.

"We didn't have to move heaven and earth to make that happen," he told us. "We just had to start being more conscious and careful [about including] our contractors in everything we did."

Nowadays, Incepture's quarterly leadership meetings include contractors, and all communication that goes to in-house staff goes to the contractors as well. They're involved in all company social events, and participate enthusiastically on the company's kickball team. They're recognized company-wide when they finish a degree, earn a certification, or receive client kudos. Contractors are fully involved in and recognized for participation in the company's charitable and community activities. And when a contractor's kid wins a state academic competition, Incepture makes a big deal of it, just as they would if the achiever belonged to a corporate staffer.

Franklin wants to develop long-term relationships with Incepture's contractors, something that distinguishes Incepture from so many other providers in the same industry. He tells his contractors, "I want you to know that we are your employer. We want you to know that you're a part of us. If you're the kind of contractor who wants to make five dollars an hour more, we'll wish you well every time that opportunity comes up; but you're probably not the best fit for us."

The contracting industry operates on somewhat of a continuum of employer reputations. Incepture chooses to operate at the high end of that continuum because, in Franklin's words, "We want to be an employer of choice among good contractors. And I think we are. So contractors want to come here, because they've heard they're going to have a better experience than they might have had somewhere else. This allows us to attract the 'A' players. And 'A' players attract other 'A' players. Our clients find out that we don't have anyone but 'A' players, and they want to hire our contractors. Then [something funny happens]; price doesn't seem to matter as much."

Connecting Doesn't Get Easier with Size

The shows at the [Las Vegas] Hilton are the most exciting shows I've ever done. The stage is huge, but the theater is intimate, so we can have a magnificent production and still connect with the audience.

—Barry Manilow

We've lost count of the number of CEOs of companies who have told us how much easier it used to be to stay connected with their workforce— back when their employee populations were in the double digits, rather than the hundreds or thousands. The fact is that nothing about employee engagement, or communication, or leadership at the enterprise level gets any easier as the organization grows larger. Indeed, each new face added to the payroll seems to increase the level of complexity geometrically.

To combat the natural "connection creep" that occurs inevitably as an organization grows larger, some companies have installed mechanisms specifically designed to keep communications and corporate affinity strong as they grow.

Borrowing a lesson from Walmart, growing Northern California supermarket chain Nugget Market holds employee rallies *every day*, in every store. Their aim is to prevent any panicked looks on the faces of associates whom customers call on to answer questions about the store's ever-changing merchandise and attention-grabbing offers. By way of an in-house TV network, they regularly talk to the troops about products and the value to each employee of delivering exceptional service, as well as to recognize employees who've put the company's values into practice. Staff members are quizzed on the content, and those who watch diligently can receive bonuses that go as high as $1,500.

Connecting with more than 65,000 workers worldwide is a challenge that Bombardier Aerospace tackles, in part, through its "listening cafes." These are places where senior leaders do little talking, but lots of (get *this*) listening—to employees, managers, suppliers, and shareholders. Then they actually use what they hear to better lead the company.

Technology has the potential to both facilitate and hinder connections between workers and the organization. We often counsel leaders who are wrestling with how to "better communicate" with the troops to periodically turn off the iPhone, unfriend Facebook, step out of the Twitterstream, walk right past the corporate video studio, and go out and "sit on the footlocker"—a phrase often used by one of our favorite leaders, the late Major General Melvin Zais. Those who do so report back to us about what an exhilarating and illuminating experience it is to go out and connect with the people who keep their businesses running. The reports often end with the phrase "like I used to."

In the final analysis, there's really no better way to satisfy your colleagues' need to connect than to simply sit down and have a one-on-one conversation—or what's referred to in my wife's Scottish culture as "a good chin-wag." Ask your people about what they're doing, what they're enjoying, what trouble they might be having. Listen to them talk about their family, their aspirations, their challenges, and their hopes. And yes, their work.

We're *not* talking about a performance evaluation. You should, of course, have other conversations throughout the year during which you talk specifically about the person's goals and their progress in reaching them. But every now and then, just try a conversation with no other agenda than to build the connection and strengthen the working relationship with another person. If you'd like some ideas on getting started—and maybe a little structure for the discussion—try asking something like this set of eight questions:

1. How's your job going?
2. What recent accomplishment are you most proud of?

3. What one thing do you think you could do better?

4. What help do you need to do that?

5. Tell me about one person who has been particularly helpful to you lately.

6. What one thing do you like most about working here?

7. What one thing do you like least about working here?

8. What one thing would you do differently if you were me?

The list starts with the sublimely simple and progresses through questions that take a little more courage for others to answer—and perhaps even for you to hear.

If you're going to Commit to having conversations like this, to keep the connections strong between you and those you lead, here are some closing thoughts on making this conversation as productive as possible:

1. Be prepared to be nowhere else but right there, with the person you're talking with. Turn off the cell phone (yes, there *is* an off switch), don't answer the landline, and close your e-mail client. Clear the decks—and your head.

2. Learn the meaning of the number one. You'll notice that some of the eight questions say "What one thing?" Stick to that limit. Otherwise, you'll likely be there all day. If there are other issues that need attention, schedule a time to explore them. But enforce the limit of "one thing" for the purposes of this discussion.

3. Listen, listen, listen. You're in input mode here, not output. Taking a few notes wouldn't hurt.

4. Underpromise and overdeliver. Make it clear that your intent is to get feedback, not to promise immediate changes. Question 8, in particular, might lead others to think that you'll implement all of their specific recommendations. So be honest. Unless your plan is to begin making immediate changes, sincerely thank them for their input, and then weigh it against the other reactions you get. But— and this is a big but—if you seem to be ignoring everything you hear, you'll shut down the flow, and quickly. When your followers see positive changes that are based on their input, your credibility—and effectiveness as a real leader—will soar.

5. Finally, have fun with this. This conversation should be seen as a good one, a chance to make a personal connection—anything but a chewing out. Your employees are taking a risk if they're completely honest with you, so play with that a little. Thank them for it. And then, act on what they tell you.

Chapter Summary

1. Making meaningful connections with people at work determines, in large part, their willingness to part with discretionary effort.

2. The opportunity to connect can begin long before people come to work for you; it continues throughout the employment relationship, and beyond.

3. Staying connected doesn't get any easier as a company grows in size.

Better Practices:

1. Calling people by their names, like Marriott COO Rob Steigerwald

2. Talent connection portals at Rackspace and Bazaarvoice

3. The Ambassador Program at Consolidated Health Services

4. Building of affinity with contracted workers at Incepture

5. Nugget Market's in-store TV telecasts from senior leadership

6. Bombardier Aerospace's listening cafes

7. Eight questions for a good employee conversation

A Case for Some Useful Benefits

A good job is more than just a paycheck. A good job fosters independence and discipline, and contributes to the health of the community. A good job is a means to provide for the health and welfare of your family, to own a home, and save for retirement.

—James H. Douglas

You'll quickly find when reading the various lists of great employer rankings that most cite a litany of perks, benefits, and amenities that these organizations offer—yet scarcely mention the other qualities and characteristics that distinguish them as outstanding workplaces. Fair enough. These things are highly visible and easy to feature in a magazine, blog, or website. Most readers can easily grasp the value of advantages such as on-site child care centers and gyms, vision coverage, and free meals. But to focus exclusively on the perks themselves, without considering what's behind them, provides only a surface understanding of these organizations' characters. This gives short shrift to the sound business-oriented rationale that compels many (not all) of them to invest good money in the benefits they provide.

For example, we could write an entire book about the legendary perks at Google, except that it's already been done, more than once. But you can be sure that a highly data-driven company like Google has studied and analyzed every one of their worker "apps," as some might call them, for efficacy, return on investment, and the ability to contribute toward their goal of assembling the best tech minds on the planet. Their famous all-day free food helps fuel those minds with better-than-average nutrition and makes it a no-brainer to stay in the office, where they can get more work done than if they were to venture off campus to eat. Same goes for the laundry rooms, haircuts, and car washes. "The goal is to strip away everything that gets in our employees' way," says executive chairman Eric Schmidt. "Let's face it: programmers want to program; they don't want to do their laundry. So we make it easy for them to do both."[1]

In our view, the best employee benefits—the whole enchilada of perks, amenities, and traditional benefits—are those that:

- Help you compete most effectively for the best talent
- Make your employees more productive
- Advance your organization's mission and values
- Are practical and cost-effective

We *don't* think benefits should be offered

- To take the place of social institutions
- For the sake of merely *sounding* progressive
- Without a solid understanding of the ROI, whether that return be measured in financial terms or other things your organization and its owners value

Many of the benefits we discussed in the original version of *Contented Cows* in 1998—especially those geared toward providing healthful lifestyles, family friendliness, or greater workplace flexibility—were considered on the cutting edge, as employers were trying hard to win the war for talent. Even Casual Fridays were thought of as somewhat avant-garde. Yet within a fairly short time, many benefits, such as fitness centers and flexible work schedules, became staples—almost entitlements. Soon, no one who wanted to work anywhere "cool" would have considered joining an employer that didn't offer a pretty full goodie bag. Then, as the economy tanked and jobs became less plentiful, just some semblance of job security was considered a "cool" benefit, and some of the extras were put away for more prosperous times. The best by-product of this exercise was that some of the less useful and quirkier perks (our favorite was "Bring your pet to work") fell by the wayside.

Before going any further, we first want to address the elephant that occupies a large corner of any room in which a discussion of employee benefits ensues within the confines of the United States: health care. Even if you're reading this but live and work outside the United States, you may find the discussion useful, so we'd suggest that you read on.

Is There a Doctor in the House?

The United States has been grappling with the great health care debate for more than two decades, since before the controversial and ill-fated plan that then First Lady Hillary Rodham Clinton proposed in 1993. The good news was that Mrs. Clinton put the topic front and center and made us look squarely into the face of a broken system with no viable future. But even after the Patient Protection and Affordable Care Act of 2010 (PPACA)—also known as Obamacare—passed, we continue to question:

1. Who should be covered by health care insurance, and to what degree?
2. Who should pay for it, and to what degree?
3. To what extent is health care a right versus a responsibility?
4. What role, if any, should government play?
5. To what extent should we expect or count on free markets to meet our needs?
6. Should individuals be lawfully required to purchase coverage?
7. What systemic improvements are required to deliver better health outcomes more efficiently?
8. How will those changes be financed?

Health care and health insurance are, at once, a social policy issue, a constitutional issue (in some countries), and a personal issue. They are also a business issue, for a host of reasons:

1. Generally speaking, people in the United States get health insurance coverage—if they have it at all—from their employer or the government. Employers are by far the most common providers of coverage for those who haven't yet hit retirement age. In 2010, 58.7 percent of that population had employment-based health benefits, down from 69.3 percent in 2000.[2]

2. The employer cost of providing worker coverage creates an average of about a $3/hour cost overhang. Since most foreign competitors don't bear this burden, it puts U.S. employers at a distinct disadvantage. Already approximating 16 percent of the gross domestic product, the cost of U.S. health care is increasing at a rate of nearly 10 percent annually.[3]

3. Based on what we know today, the PPACA will allow employers to be able to offload this obligation beginning in 2014 by *paying a fine and throwing covered employees into state insurance pools*. Although they're encouraged to do the opposite, it is still a very real possibility—which will give us yet another way to distinguish between employers of choice and the others.

4. Without extreme pressure from patients and payors, and the invention of a new business model, health care providers will never graduate from the costly and inefficient fee-for-service system.

So why is this an issue with respect to worker engagement and productivity?

Providing workers with access to health care at more affordable group rates is one of the last bastions of the old social contract in the employment arena. Because of runaway cost increases and the continued fraying of the social fabric in the workplace, many employers are deciding that they either cannot or will not afford to retain coverage for their people. Even those that *do* are rebalancing the cost-sharing arrangement. Witness the fact that only 14 of *Fortune's* "100 Best Companies to Work For" in 2012 (e.g., Zappos, Boston Consulting Group, and NuStar Energy) currently pay 100 percent of employees' health care premiums, down from 21 percent on the 2008 list. And these are among the very *best* places to work. Of far greater importance than the exact nature of the cost-sharing arrangement (and users *should* pick up part of the tab) is the fact that when it comes to our increasing health care expense, we as a nation are like the slow-boiled laboratory frog. For good and compelling reasons, employers don't want—and simply can't afford—to be the last frog in the pot.

Yet, like Robert Owen, the nineteenth-century mill owner referenced in Chapter 1, we also cannot afford to find ourselves with a workforce that is increasingly dispirited, distracted, and unreliable because they lack reasonable access to competent medical care. One of the greatest dangers we face as leaders is the loss of customer focus, fresh ideas, productivity, and safety that is associated with distracted workers. I'm certainly going to be distracted on the job if I've got a health condition that I can't afford to have treated properly or am worried about one of my relative's well-being. So we all have skin in this game whether we want to or not.

What to Do

Although each management needs to figure out what is best for their organization, we would recommend that everyone give serious consideration to the following while making these decisions:

- Become much more knowledgeable about the various facets of the delivery of health services, and the economics thereof, both in general and with respect to your organization.

- Resist the temptation to base your decisions about participation in this arena purely—or even largely—on narrow, short-term factors. Instead, take a 360-degree look at it from 39,000 feet while considering all stakeholders, and then decide.

- Join with like-minded employers to shape the debate, and more important, the solutions.

- Don't wait, because time is not on your side.

There are lots of ways that employers can address their workforce's health care needs without paying for all or part of their insurance premiums.

A growing trend that makes a lot of sense for many organizations is to "insource" the health care of employees and their dependents. In other words, the companies install full service medical clinics on-site that are staffed with primary care physicians and even full staffs of other medical professionals in some cases. Organizations as diverse as SAS Institute, the Pebble Beach Company, and the City of Clearwater, Florida, have seen substantial improvements in both cost and quality of care by taking this approach. Factor in the convenience and the added connection that on-site health care can form between employee and employer, and such a benefit creates a certain "stickiness" that weighs heavily in an employee's decision to leave one employer for another not equally equipped.

Increasing the portion of health care coverage that employees must pay is not the only evidence that employers are asking employees to assume a greater share of the responsibility for their own health. Smart employers are partnering with workers to make it easier for employees to *be* healthier and to be less in need of the costly resources required to fix problems once they happen.

Wegmans Supermarkets, with more than 80 stores in five northeastern states and a long and distinguished reputation as an employer of choice, has practically made employee health a religion. For the past several years, the company has facilitated annual employee participation in the Eat Well, Live Well Challenge, which includes a system to increase exercise, quit smoking, and enjoy a healthier diet. In 2011, more than 11,000 (about a third) of their employees took the challenge, which for Wegmans means more than simply putting a poster on the wall of the break room. Stores organized walks and provided participants with free pedometers. Managers served as good examples and led the campaigns in many locations, and employees were recognized for their achievements.

Louisiana's Ochsner Health Systems offers reductions of up to $2,000 off employee health care premiums for employees who exercise regularly. The company is one of more than 120 employers that hire Virgin HealthMiles, owned by British magnate Sir Richard Branson to monitor employees' daily exercise. HealthMiles distributes devices such as accelerometers to measure employees' activity. The company estimates that every dollar invested in the reward program yields $3 to $6 in health care savings. Talk about ROI!

Adults Only, Please

With the exception of the relatively small segment of the legal working population comprised of teenagers in part-time jobs, we're going to assume that most of us are hiring adults to do the work that sustains our enterprises. And that's precisely why it's crucial to treat those people like the grown-ups they are.

Contented Cow employers establish clear performance goals and then provide the wherewithal to achieve those goals. They spend a lot less time worrying about the hours people come to work and leave, how many days they work and don't work, and whether or not they should be paid while they're at home preventing the spread of whatever communicable disorder they picked up from a coworker who felt an obligation (financial or otherwise) to come to work, germs and all.

After addressing the issue of health care, employees want workplace benefits that simply make life, at work and away, a little easier and more manageable, while still allowing them to get their jobs done. This is especially true for workers juggling the responsibilities of work and family, often for multiple generations. The phenomenon of the "sandwich generation"—in which workers must care not only for their children but for their aging parents as well—has expanded to what one woman called the "club sandwich generation." In her late 40s, she told us of the physical and emotional demands associated with her middle position in a five-generation family that required her attention not only for her kids and parents, but for a young grandchild *and* a grandmother in her 90s.

It's no great revelation that providing workers with flexible schedules and the ability to work at home via technology can substantially enhance the quality of their lives. As a consequence, practices like these have the *potential* to improve the quality of their work. In fact, in an age when the boundaries between work and home are becoming increasingly blurred, it's beginning to matter increasingly less exactly when, where, and by what means you get your work done. This puts a premium on the ability of both workers and their bosses to manage relationships, priorities, and use of time.

Amerisure Mutual Insurance Company of Dallas has been a champion of both flexible and compressed work schedules and work-from-home arrangements for more than a decade. But they've been so successful with the practices in part because they ask employees to prepare a proposal that details how they'll manage their new arrangement and how they'll keep their productivity in the same range as under a more traditional model.

The risks inherent in more flexible and less tightly controlled working relationships are at least twofold. On one end of the continuum is many bosses' fear that without more traditional controls, their people won't do the same quantity and/or quality of work that they might if they were chained to an office and a clock. On the other end is the very real and present danger that workers will forget to observe a reasonable "quittin' time," to the detriment of the other parts of, and people in, their lives—an act which itself can adversely affect a person's work. The San Francisco law firm of Fenwick & West has been successful in attracting and retaining employees, many of whom are women, who might have left the firm were it not for its practices of job sharing and reduced-hour schedules (available to anyone, for any reason). But to make sure the system works for everyone, a workflow coordinator helps ensure that people on reduced schedules are indeed working those reduced schedules, without the "schedule creep" that can so easily happen, especially during busy times. They also help guard against the "out-of-sight, out-of-mind" syndrome that can befall the career aspirations of people who do much of their work without a physical presence in the office.

All in the Family

If you accept the notion that the best employee benefits are those that free people up from the encumbrances that can slow them down or cause their work quality to suffer, then it's hard to argue against the value of child care benefits. Yet it can be a complicated issue, as employers of varying sizes contemplate equally varying commitments to child care solutions for their employees. Some companies offer referral services, a practically free but frankly not very valuable service to employees. Others go to the opposite extreme by operating on-site child care facilities ranging from modest to elaborate. Still others come down somewhere in the middle by offering child care subsidies at nearby facilities. Whatever your organization decides to do about child care, if anything, you should be mindful that there is a cost associated with doing nothing.

SAS Institute has become something of a model for on-site child care, with two Montessori schools at their Cary, North Carolina, headquarters. Both are heavily subsidized to make them affordable to anyone who needs them, space permitting. And if space is *not* permitting, the company has arranged for other high-quality care nearby at even lower rates. And with employee turnover at 4 percent versus an industry average of almost 20 percent, SAS must be doing something right. Since its founding in 1976, the company has become the world's largest independent vendor in the business intelligence market and consistently wins honors for being a company full of Contented Cows.

But on-site child care isn't necessarily always the answer. Construction of a new child care center is a major capital expenditure, and most experts agree you'll need a steady supply of 75 to 100 children to make it break even. Moreover, they warn that on-site child care is often the only alternative considered and then often rejected because of the cost and impracticality. On the other hand, companies with excess building capacity—due to downsizing or increased telecommuting—may find that a child care center is a great use for empty space they already own.

Years ago, I worked for a small software developer whose chief accountant gave birth to a healthy baby girl and returned to work a few weeks later with the child in tow—and not just for a visit. I was surprised at how completely unobtrusive the child's presence was in the office. Little did I know that that woman was at the head of a trend that's growing in organizations with mostly smaller, less formal work environments.

Beginning in 2000, Schools Financial Credit Union of Sacramento, California, has encouraged mothers and fathers to bring their babies to work for the entire workday—either until the child is six months old or begins to crawl, whichever comes first. (We don't even want to think about it without that stipulation!) Vice president of marketing Nathan Schmidt claims, "Babies actually cause few distractions." Companies like Schools Financial Credit Union, Badger Healthy Body Care Products, and others find that parents return to work earlier under the plan, and it's cheaper for the company than hiring temps or training replacement workers. In most cases, everyone—employee, employer, and coworkers—understands that the worker may not be contributing 100 percent (and compensation may reflect that), but it may still be a viable option. Clearly, it's not for every employer or every employee, but it's one more example of employers doing what works, for the benefit both of the organization and its members.

Programs, Programs, Get Your Programs

Don't let the number, variety, and complexity of the various family-oriented programs cause you to lose sight of the fact that they *can* make a difference—IF your employees consider them valuable; IF they reduce stress, turnover, hiring, training, and replacement costs; and IF they allow people to get more done and better serve customers. But don't limit your thinking to those areas. Recognize that many people are in family circumstances as a matter of choice, but some are not. Organizations will likely have more success with family responsiveness if they ask and expect employees to take responsibility for their own family issues and then partner with them to provide ways to address family needs. Companies that opt instead to take responsibility for all their employees' family choices will both fail at it and regret their choice.

As with so many things in the workplace, and in life, the best advice on how to provide benefits is to simply *ask*. Ask your employees, "What are you struggling with all the time? What would make your life easier? So much easier that it would enable you to make a substantially greater contribution to what we do here?" If you have more than about 100 or so employees, you may want to ask those questions via a well-managed and well-designed employee survey. But if your population's smaller than that, just go out and ask them.

Caring Can't Be Legislated

The United States—and to an even greater extent, other countries—have enacted volumes of legislation in an attempt to compel employers to treat current and potential employees "right," with respect to hiring, working conditions, separation, and other matters of employment. One reason for so many laws is, of course, that more than a few have failed to treat people this way without a little legislative encouragement.

Laws like the Americans with Disabilities Act of 1990 (ADA) and the Family and Medical Leave Act of 1993 (FMLA) mandated some of the practices that many employers had been using for years, without anyone telling them they had to. Unfortunately, they are practices that many others still creatively skirt, even in the presence of the legislation. At the same time, and because the application of legal standards is sometimes a messy affair, the law of unintended consequences has emerged in many cases. This has caused undue hardships on employers and has limited opportunities for the very people—workers—the laws were meant to protect.

One employer that doesn't seem to need much governmental guidance around issues like this is, in fact, a government entity itself. The City of Lakeway, Texas, about a half hour drive from Austin, has a long history of making its own employment decisions in ways that seem to work for the city and for the people who work for its residents. Serving a population of slightly more than 11,000 people (according to the 2010 census) with a small staff, the city managers have shown outstanding compassion, pragmatism, and wisdom when it comes to handling employees with serious illnesses.

There was one case of a new employee who learned after working for only one month that he needed an immediate operation. Rather than release or replace him, they held his spot open and encouraged him to return to work when he was able. He's now been a productive and appreciative member of the municipal staff for 13 years. Another Lakeway employee was diagnosed with cancer and given no realistic chance for survival beyond a few months. Although there was no "policy" or even a precedent for telecommuting, the managers set her up with the technology in her home to let her work remotely for the last eight months of her life. Reasonable accommodation—or caring innovation? Who knows? But the result was eight more months of productivity, and in all likelihood, a several month extension of the woman's life.

These are not isolated incidents in Lakeway. Most recently, a new department director was hired but diagnosed with a treatable cancer before she started work and needed an immediate operation and chemotherapy. Although some managers would have exercised their right to rescind the employment offer, the managers in Lakeway granted her a delayed start date and welcomed her to the team after she'd successfully completed her treatment.

There's something more going on here than the obvious benefit to the involved workers. People in both your organization and most others are watching and carefully noting how people are treated when they're going through a rough time. They often quietly wonder, "What would happen if that were me?" We suspect that there's a lot less worrying and a lot more work going on in the City of Lakeway offices than in places where there's not such a solid precedent.

People often pose questions about paid vacation, sick leave, and parental leave when we're asked to speak or write about Contented Cow employers. Many of our international friends and clients are surprised to learn that U.S. law doesn't mandate paid maternity leave, for example. Still, many employers—especially larger ones—do typically provide something in the range of four to six weeks' paid leave for qualifying mothers. Whether or not paid parental leave *should* be required by law is a discussion for another context. However, it's hard to argue against the practice as a source of competitive distinction among employers vying for talent, Commitment, and engagement.

According to a 2012 Rutgers University study, new mothers with paid leave are 93 percent more likely to be working 9 to 12 months after the birth than those without it.[4] This suggests that a lot of sleep-deprived mothers may be returning to work too soon, for perceived economic reasons, only to throw in the towel a few months down the road. As fathers who only *attended* the births of our children rather than participating more fully, and whose wives spent *far* more time than we did taking care of midnight feedings, we can only imagine what it must be like to Commit oneself to a job before the body and emotions are ready to make a comeback.

Just as the City of Lakeway didn't have to extend these considerations to the employees we mentioned, Genentech (now part of Roche) isn't required—either by law or social norm—to provide 10 weeks of fully paid maternity leave to its U.S. workers. However, it does. The FMLA stipulates 12 weeks of *job-protected* leave, none of which has to be with pay; yet General Mills extends that to 26 weeks, with a portion of the leave (the amount depending on a number of factors) at full pay. And while Boston Consulting Group certainly isn't compelled by law to provide a full three months' paid maternity leave, the practice may be partially responsible for the company's 19 percent turnover rate in a pressure cooker industry known for churning roughly a third of its workforce in a given year.

Although there is absolutely no legal requirement to do so, Discovery Communications—which owns the Discovery Channel, TLC, and Animal Planet, among other things—gives its employees a generous allowance for paid caregiving leave. This allows workers to deal with the illness or incapacitation of just about any family member. As the workforce and entire population ages, Discovery and other companies with a similar benefit have seen a steady rise in the use of this kind of leave to care for parents and even aging spouses.

Even where paid leave *is* mandated by law, some employers choose to top up the required allowance to something a little more generous. In Canada, where most employers must provide 15 weeks of paid maternity leave, Yukon Hospital Corporation goes beyond that to offer up to 17 *additional* weeks at up to 93 percent of regular salary. And it's not only birth mothers who get the perk; they offer the same deal to fathers and adoptive parents.[5] This is doubtlessly one of the reasons Yukon was named one of Canada's "Top 100 Employers" for 2012.

The U.S. government has also refrained from getting involved in mandating (or even suggesting) sick pay. Although it's common practice, it seems fundamentally stupid to ask people to come to work when they're sick—especially when working can reasonably be expected to prolong their recovery, and most certainly when there's a chance they can spread their illness to others. At the same time, three predictable consequences of requiring people to forego compensation while they're sick at home are:

1. They won't be sick at home; they'll be sick at work.
2. They'll be worried—that is, distracted (key word)—lest they become sick.
3. They'll form a clear opinion about how much you care (another key word) about people as human beings, and that opinion won't accrue to your credit.

Bon Voyage, Vacation Policy

Netflix made quite a splash a few years ago when people learned that the online DVD and streaming video purveyor doesn't have a vacation policy for its salaried workers. That's right. No vacation policy. It's not that people don't get any paid vacation; it's just that the company simply hasn't complicated the matter with an "official" policy. Employees can take as much time off as they like, whenever they want, provided they get their work done and their boss knows when they'll be away. Known for its high-performance culture (okay, there was that ill-conceived price hike, and the Qwikster debacle—but hey, nobody's perfect), Netflix doesn't suffer slackers. In fact, the careers of those deemed merely "adequate" are more likely to be a short subject than a feature film.

The company acknowledges that everyone's a professional in its statement that "we don't measure people by how many evenings or weekends they are in the cube. We do try to measure people by how much, how quickly, and how well they get work done—especially under deadline."

Netflix isn't the only one. Bazaarvoice, the customer review software company we introduced in Chapter 8, has the same deal. According to Recruitment Marketing Guy Ryan Hand, "For real, anyone can take any amount of time, or not, that they want. We find that 99 percent of our people don't abuse the system at all, and the 1 percent [who do] get a refresher on how it works. We all have [to get our work done], and it's up to us to produce. The company saves a ton of money not having to track it all, and it gives everyone a sense of independence that Bazaarvoice treated them like adults."

It's hard to quantify the return on the investment in employee benefits in some cases (whether of the innovative or more traditional variety), yet those numbers are pretty clear in others. But there are plenty of successful companies who have both quantifiable and anecdotal evidence that has convinced them they were doing the smart thing for the success of the enterprise. Some examples:

Ever eat a Clif Bar? If so, someone who had a hand in making it likely rode a $500 commuter bike to work, compliments of the popular food and energy product maker. Clif Bar workers who carpool, ride bikes, use public transit, or walk to work earn points toward a maximum of $960 in annual rewards. Employees can get a $6,500 contribution toward the purchase of a car with a hybrid, biodiesel, or natural gas engine. When you know that the company's "Five Aspirations" are "Sustaining our planet, community, people, business, and brands," it all fits. And something that fits J.M. Smucker's value of a highly educated workforce is 100 percent tuition reimbursement, offered as it is at Smucker, for any degree, with practically no limits.

Plamex has long taken a practical approach to employee perks and services. The company that lobbied the Mexican government to change laws requiring an original birth certificate to get a marriage license brings the Baja California Department of Motor Vehicles into the factory one day a month to process employees' driver's license renewals. Think about how big a hero you would be if you eliminated your employees' need to stand in line for hours at *their* local DMV! And the company also provides on-site parenting classes (how to function well as a parent, not how to become one) to anyone in the plant who wishes to attend. Says company HR director Diana Alvarado, "When things are going well at home, we find people come to work, they come on time, and they do better work." Makes perfect sense to us.

And speaking of how well things are going at home, it's clear that unstable employment of a spouse is a distraction for the working partner in any couple that relies on two incomes—which is just about everyone these days. But companies in certain professions, such as health care and information technology (IT), have found that having an unemployed spouse or partner is a relatively strong predictor of reluctant resignations from employees who follow the other breadwinner to a job in another city. This impacts health care and IT because jobs in those fields are generally more plentiful and found in almost any part of the country. So it's more than altruism—indeed, a sharp sense of practicality—that drives Bon Secour Richmond Health Systems to provide free seminars on job searches and interviewing for unemployed family members of its 21,000 employees.

Salt Lake City–based mail order provider of contact lenses 1-800-CONTACTS has also taken this kind of caring approach. Recognizing that the past few years have taken both a financial and an emotional toll on lots of people—and again, wanting to minimize significant distractions—the company makes available one-time emergency financial assistance to any employee in a crisis. And you don't have to have a big HR department, a formal policy—or even 850 employees, as CONTACTS does—to reap the benefits of extending random acts of grace and kindness to the people who work with you. We know of so many examples in which leaders reached into their pockets or wrote out a check to help an employee in need—not because they had to, but because they could. Were some on the other end of a scam? Maybe one or two; but the vast majority never forgot the feeling of giving help to someone who needed and deserved it and whose work would forever be evidence that they never forgot the act of kindness.

Chapter Summary

1. If you care about your people, you provide benefits that are truly beneficial—to you, to them, and to your bottom line. You focus on benefits that:
   o Help you compete most effectively for the best talent.
   o Help make your employees more productive.
   o Advance your organization's mission and values.
   o Are practical and cost-effective.

2. Getting and paying for health care in the United States continues to be a major and largely unresolved issue. The current system, in which employers pay for the bulk of health care, gives us an unsustainable labor cost disadvantage and provides neither the best nor most efficient outcomes. The trend is for employers to shift both financial and behavioral responsibility for health from themselves to their employees.

3. Contented Cow employers treat their employees like adults with respect to sick time, family leave, and vacation.

4. Generally speaking, benefits plans work better when responsible leaders thoughtfully consider and enact solutions rather than waiting to be forced to do so by legislation or disengaged workers.

5. Some of the best employee benefits are those that reduce employee distractions and help people focus more clearly on their work.

Better Practices:

1. In-house medical clinics (SAS Institute, the Pebble Beach Company, and the City of Clearwater, Florida)

2. The "Eat Well, Live Well Challenge" at Wegmans Supermarkets

3. On-site child care at SAS Institute

4. The flexible and compassionate practices of the City of Lakeway, Texas

5. No vacation policy at Netflix and Bazaarvoice

6. One-time crisis financial assistance at 1-800-CONTACTS

Contented Cows
Are Enabled

CHAPTER

10

Empower This!

We've got to take out the boss element.
—Jack Welch, former CEO, General Electric

The Etymology of a Buzzword

In a speech that I originally gave in New York in August 1979, I used a word that I had never before heard used within the context of employee relations. Yet over the past three decades, the use of that same word in the business lexicon has reached virus-like proportions. In the process, the term has taken on a life (and many new definitions) of its own. Sadly, as is often the case with any product, image, or even an humble word that somehow makes the journey from obscurity to ubiquity, we see entire books, seminars, podcasts, lectures, T-shirts, and ball caps devoted to it. There's nothing wrong with that—except perhaps for the fact that with every mindless repetition, its meaning gets hopelessly muddled, if not lost altogether. That word is *empowered*.

The reason for discussing empowerment now is even more crucial than it was back then. While everyone rushes around doing whatever they do to "empower" their people, many are proceeding entirely in the wrong direction. And if you think about it, you might realize that your people may not really need empowering at all. After all, they know how to find their way to work, what their jobs are, and probably the best ways of doing them.

Management professor Henry Mintzberg offers perhaps the best analogy when he tells us to consider a truly advanced social system: the beehive. Queen bees don't empower worker bees. The worker bees are "adults" who know exactly what they have to do. Indeed, the queen bee has no role in the genuinely strategic decisions of the hive, such as the one to move on to a new location. The bees decide collectively, responding to the informative dances of the scouts. What the queen bee does is exude a chemical substance that holds the system together. She is responsible for what has been called the spirit of the hive.[1]

Similarly, our experience has shown that what most employees really need is for managers to stop standing on their necks long enough to let them *do* their jobs! In short, what they need is for us to stop *disempowering* them. And the difference, we assure you, is more than semantic.

Eerily similar to the thesis of this book, a pivotal concept of those remarks back in 1979 was that successful organizations went to truly great lengths to ensure that they were hiring only those who were qualified for the position in question and equipped by virtue of temperament, ideology, and attitude to be successful and content within the organization. After establishing that vital first step, it was then equally important to ensure that these spanking new, highly qualified, and motivated troops knew the organization's whys and wherefores and were firmly pointed to a target. Crack troops don't tolerate standing at parade rest or aimless wandering very well. In fact, they become dangerous—both to themselves and those around them.

To be effective, these folks need to be led by managers who understand and skillfully articulate the mission (they're good with crayons). They must be scrupulously fair; able to tread the line between bullying and being chicken; genuinely care about their people; and, not unlike the queen bee, know that their own principal duty is to support the organization.

Although these prerequisites are vital to building and maintaining a high-performance organization, they are simply not enough. There's still another step—one that, if not taken, will soon find you facing a bunch of extremely talented, highly motivated, capably led, and *very* frustrated people.

The Next Step

We've got to make sure our people are totally and completely equipped to do their jobs. Then—and only then—can we get ourselves (and the organization) out of their way. Stand aside and let them work!

The good news is that—contrary to what many currently popular books and seminars espouse—this is not something you do *to* your people, and it's certainly not something you can achieve on command. The *bad* news, as so many organizations have learned, is that you really do have to do it—fully, completely, and without equivocation or you'll regret it later. You can't just talk about it or "kinda" do it. You either do it or you don't.

We're not suggesting that getting people to assume additional responsibility is altogether easy. It's not. Some folks *like* being told what to do—and not just those in the lower echelons. But the real problem is that too many managers enjoy satisfying that wish. And because they enjoy it, they're good at it. They start by hiring people who *need* to be told what to do, and then tell them in every way imaginable that they don't want them to think for themselves or take responsibility. Requiring people to be accountable for their work and allowing them to define and solve problems requires them to amend both their roles and expectations.

Identifying Four Types of Managers

During his legendary and highly successful tenure at the helm of General Electric, Jack Welch—and the others on his executive leadership team—formulated a matrix to describe the full range of managers in the organization. This matrix applies to nearly every other organization we've ever encountered. Born of the recognition that the ideals of involvement and excitement and turning people loose didn't always match the reality of life in GE, the company used this "Four Types of Managers" model throughout Welch's tenure, which ended in 2001. It successfully helped leaders throughout GE more closely align their leadership styles and practices with the company's stated values.

The problem, as Welch and his team saw it, was that some of the company's leaders—including managers at all levels—remained unwilling or unable to abandon big-company, big-shot autocracy and embrace the values that GE was trying to foster. Following is the model—the Four Types—which we've adapted here ever so slightly, to put into Contented Cows terms:

GE's Four Types of Managers

Type I [the Contented Cow] not only delivers on performance commitments but believes in and furthers GE's small-company values. This group's trajectory is onward and upward, and the men and women who comprise it will represent the core of our senior leadership into the next century.

Type II [the Slow Milker, Chronic Kicker, or Finicky Eater] does not meet commitments, share our values—or last long at GE.

Type III [the Fence-Breaking Explorer] believes in the values but sometimes misses commitments. We encourage taking swings, and Type III is typically given another chance.

Type IV [the Low-Producing Boss Cow]. The calls on the first two types are easy. Type III takes some judgment; but Type IV is the most difficult. One is always tempted to avoid taking action, because Type IVs deliver short-term results. But they do so without regard to values and, in fact, often diminish them by squeezing, stifling, and grinding people down. Some of these [at GE] learned to change; most couldn't. The decision to begin removing Type IVs was a watershed—the ultimate test of our ability to walk the talk. However, we had to do it if we wanted GE people to be open, to speak up, to share, and to act boldly outside traditional lines of authority and functional boxes in this new learning, sharing environment.[2]

One Bad Apple Can Spoil the Whole Barrel

Hundreds, if not thousands, of contenders abound in the wings, waiting to accept the accolades and indeed the full financial rewards associated with Contented Cow stature. But many of these companies fail to progress beyond the "wannabe" stage. This can often be the fault of a few—even just one—of the aforementioned Type IV managers. These few "bad apples" manage to water down—if not completely obliterate—legitimate Contented Cow managers' efforts.

Look around. Maybe you're feeling pretty smug about the contentedness of your workforce in general; however, you notice a pocket of your organization with uncharacteristically high turmoil and turnover. It's possible they're still making their numbers. But it might be worth taking a closer look.

In more than one company we've examined, we've seen the valiant efforts of lots of well-intentioned leaders be completely overshadowed by one or two Low-Producing (or even High-Producing) Boss Cows. But because these Type IVs were achieving short-term results—albeit at the expense of people in their areas—it was tough for anyone to summon the courage to do anything about it.

It's not just the damage these Type IVs do within their own departments. Greater destruction by far occurs elsewhere in the organization, when people see managers tolerating or even encouraging this type of behavior. Their mixed message seems to be: "Our people are our most valuable assets. Really, they are. And our practice is to treat people in ways that will motivate them to stellar performance. We realize we've got one or two managers around here who don't get it. That's okay, because they're turning in the needed results right now. If you're not under their control, don't worry about them. Just be glad you don't work for them. If you do happen to work for them . . . well . . . it's a free world."

Guess what? That approach just won't work. The glaring inconsistency involving even just a few will undermine and mitigate the majority's valiant efforts. Once again, it is an all-or-nothing proposition. You're either Committed or you aren't. This isn't a quest for the moral high ground. It's just plain good business. Every one of our Contented Cow companies detailed in Chapter 1 works pretty hard to encourage, recognize, and develop the Type Is in their midst and to send the Type IIs and IVs to work somewhere else—preferably for a competitor.

If you discover a couple of these folks in your organization, you owe it to them (and everyone else) to be very clear about your commitment to these principles. If they choose not to sign on, cull them from the herd—now. Do it professionally and humanely, but do it!

Give People Back Their Work

As currently viewed, "empowerment" is something that we bestow upon those whose boxes on the organization chart are south of our own. This plantation mind-set therefore implies that they wouldn't have this power if we didn't grant it to them. Contrast that with some situations where the workers truly *do* have a high degree of influence (control, if you will) over their work and the work environment. Two that come readily to mind are those involving commercial airline pilots and professional basketball players. In both cases, the workers are perfectly well empowered already, with no thanks to either a manager or any sort of "empowerment program."

January 15, 2009. US Airways flight 1549. Most of us remember the so-called Miracle on the Hudson, in which Captain Chesley "Sully" Sullenberger successfully "landed" the Airbus A320 he was piloting on the surface of the Hudson River after a flock of geese flew into and shut down both of the jet's engines shortly after takeoff from New York's LaGuardia Airport. I remember it especially clearly because I happened to be relaxing in LaGuardia's Delta Sky Club at the moment it happened. As my delayed flight had been scheduled to take off at the precise minute that flight 1549 *did* take off, it's never been lost on me that those could have been *my* geese and Sully *wouldn't* have been my pilot.

The success of this feat—in which no one was killed, or even seriously injured—was due in no small part to Sully's training and skill not only as an Airbus captain but as an experienced glider pilot. But a large measure of the credit has to go to what we've been talking about in this chapter. The captain didn't worry about whether or not he was "empowered" to put the plane down on the river between two bridges and a host of skyscrapers. The cockpit voice recordings make it very clear that he never once tried to contact his boss to ask *permission* to do so, and he *certainly* never checked to see if the company had a policy governing this kind of catastrophe. He was *enabled* by virtue of the job and the attendant responsibility to do whatever it took to save the lives of the 155 passengers.

And can you imagine Los Angeles Lakers coach Mike Brown calling a special practice or a time-out during a game for the purpose of empowering Kobe Bryant to pass the ball, take a shot, or run a different play than the one that had been called? Of course not—and the reason is that whatever empowering is going on took place long ago, when it was "baked" into the person's job.

By contrast, a position that used to convey considerable latitude but that has been recently *dis*empowered is that of physician. Owing to the emergence of managed, er, mangled, care, physicians find themselves being micromanaged by insurance company bureaucrats who have nowhere near their level of medical training—and have certainly never held a patient's life in their hands. A 15-minute conversation with your primary care physician will likely confirm that he or she doesn't like this—and they certainly don't find that it enhances either business outcomes or the quality of care they are able to provide for patients.

No profit grows where is no pleasure ta'en . . .

—William Shakespeare

Chapter Summary

1. Stop trying to "empower" your people. You'll only drive them (and yourself) crazy trying to figure out how to do it. It's far easier and more beneficial to eradicate those things that serve to *dis*empower them (dumb policies and procedures, managerial behaviors, etc.)— and to do it with a vengeance!

2. Hire people who truly want to take responsibility for their work; then get out of their way.

3. As painful as it may be in the short run, either convert the Boss Cows to a new style of management or help them find a new job . . . preferably with a competitor.

Enabled Employees Are Incredibly Well Trained

To try to build an organization against weakness frustrates the purpose of organization.

—Peter Drucker

Take a look inside the cockpit, er, flight deck, of a modern jetliner and marvel for a moment at what you see—the gauges, computers, screens, levers, dials, and everything that makes up the mind-boggling array of gizmos, every one of which serves an importance purpose. But then notice what you *don't* see: namely, a supervisor or manager. Instead, there are two people who, due to the vagaries of crew scheduling, probably don't know each other very well. But they *do* know exactly what their job is and how to do it.

For those who need a numbers fix about now, consider this. In terms of the ratio of worker bees per manager, commercial airline pilots are among the most productive employees you'll find anywhere. For the major commercial carriers, the number of crew members per manager is greater than 100:1. Compare that with the span of control ratio in your (or most any other) business!

So how did they reach such high efficiency? Besides having a well-defined mission and crystal clear goals, they do what they do because they have a commitment to training that is unmatched by just about any other profession.

Mind you, it's not that the airlines necessarily *want* to spend exorbitant amounts of time and money to train their aircrews to this degree of proficiency. They know they *have* to, because nobody in their right mind would get on the plane without it. Moreover, they are compelled by law to meet certain safety requirements. The problem with our more earthbound organizations is that we don't have anybody or anything scaring us enough to make us do it.

Again, US Airways flight 1549 comes to mind. When we're trying to pound home the importance of training during a speech or seminar, all we have to do is flash on the screen that familiar image of more than 100 passengers balanced precariously, but relatively unharmed, on the wings of the Airbus, floating in the Hudson River—and our point is made.

But you know the drill. Most companies fund training efforts during periods of prosperity, but inevitably reduce their training and development budget as soon as business starts to slow. Witness the reduction in training during and shortly after the great recession. According to data from the American Society for Training and Development (ASTD), the average per person training investment of the Fortune Global 500 companies dropped by a third, from $1,616 in 2005 to $1,067 in 2010.[1] Although ASTD believes (hopes?) that organizations' commitment to training is on the upswing, incalculable damage was done during the training drought associated with those years. As a result, we now have legions of workers—and their leaders—for whom learning and development has largely been a do-it-yourself affair.

Think for a moment about the sheer stupidity of this concept: we have an earnings problem, so we're going to work our way out of it by dumbing down the organization with less skilled, less competent people. Now the only problem will be to find customers dumb enough to purchase our goods and services, and even dumber investors to buy our stock!

Training Expands the Meaning of Professionalism

Where is it written that just because they don't wear lab coats or epaulets or attend Harvard, a bartender, machinist, sales clerk, assembly worker, or anyone else should not be viewed and treated as a professional—with all the attendant rights, privileges, and responsibilities? We're advocating that if you really want to maximize your employees' level of contribution, you treat them the same way the hospital does its doctors, the airline its pilots, the law firm its lawyers, and so forth. In short, you treat them as the professionals they are.

An investment in knowledge always pays the best interest.
—Benjamin Franklin

The aforementioned ASTD study reports that American organizations provided an average of 32 hours of training per year per employee in 2010.[2] Contented Cow Companies tend to invest considerably more. Chesapeake Energy, for example, provides an average of 54 hours of training per employee per year. General Mills does better than that with 75 hours; Marriott provides 89 hours a year; and NuStar Energy comes in at a whopping 110 hours!

Chick-fil-A, the Atlanta-based chain that sold more than 282 million of their signature chicken sandwiches from more than 1,600 stores in 2011, is as serious about training and lifelong learning as they are about serving the best chicken sandwich in the country. Lest you think running a profitable quick-service restaurant is a simple matter, consider that this company—with better than $4 billion in annual revenues—regularly sends managers to executive education programs at Wharton, the Harvard Business School, Columbia University, and more than a dozen other schools.

We've all seen this classic scenario: someone is technically very proficient in her job, so we naturally assume that she'll be able to lead and inspire others to do great work. So, one Friday afternoon, we call her into the office and say, "Congratulations! You're a manager now. You start on Monday, and you've got all weekend to get ready." Not so at Chick-fil-A. One of the company's most distinguishing qualities is their ability to recognize that leadership is a profession and, as such, is worthy of the same preparation as any other.

"As soon as someone's job changes from that of an individual contributor to a 'people leader,'" said Phil Orazi, senior director of training and development at Chick-fil-A, "they begin a yearlong 'leader onboarding' process." The program includes an extensive educational component, since—contrary to what some believe—people *can* learn to lead and can continue to do so by regularly assessing the leader's skills and practices. Throughout the year, the new leader receives support via one-on-one coaching from more experienced leaders.

Having interacted over the course of two decades with various members of their senior leadership and corporate staff, we can say that this strong emphasis on leadership training—and professionalism—shows in everything Chick-fil-A does. It also puts them a notch above so many others in their industry.

The Hidden Costs of Ignored Training

Let's look for a moment beyond the obvious benefits of training to the cost of *not* providing needed training. We understand the protests that begin, "But training is expensive." And we reply, "Yes. It can be. But have you priced incompetence lately?" The truth is that scrimping on training forces you to pay an added price for rework, lost customers, and the cost of additional supervisors to run around looking over the shoulders of marginally competent employees.

There is a cost far greater and more debilitating than any of these, however. This has to do with what happens to your employees' psyche and performance when they don't feel particularly competent or confident in their ability to do their work.

How many times in your life have you started an interaction (where you're the customer) with a sales clerk, call center operator, waiter, or someone similar who opened with the words "I'm new at this . . ."? (By the way, how would you like to hear those same words from your neurosurgeon as you're being wheeled into the operating room?) That pronouncement allows that person to essentially say to you—and more important, to themselves—"I'm probably gonna screw this up, so please be patient and understanding with me." And we all know that if someone *thinks* they will screw something up, it greatly increases the likelihood that they will! Moreover, if they screw it up *this* time, how confident are they going to be the next time? Your potentially contented, productive employee understandably just became a very demoralized one.

Make no mistake about it: people who are proficient in their jobs and who know they will be able to handle the difficult tasks ahead feel confident about themselves and stay calm and poised in on-the-spot crises. As a result, they perform better than employees who never got lessons in the basics.

Training Sends a Message

One of Howard Schultz's first acts when he returned as CEO of Starbucks in early 2008 was to pour out a bold plan to retrain his company's employees on the most basic function of their jobs—how to make and serve coffee and espresso drinks. And so on February 26 of that year, Starbucks closed all 7,100 of its U.S. stores for 3 evening hours to give a refresher course to more than 135,000 partners—in a single shot.

The "star" in Starbucks had begun to fade well into the brand's fourth decade, after years of sustained growth and popularity. Schultz believed the answer to reversing the downward trend lay not so much in new products, pricing, or branding, but in training employees to deliver that perfect shot of espresso. Not only did this represent a sizable outlay in training cost, but the lost revenue—even during the lower traffic evening hours—was enough to give Starbucks stockholders a jolt equivalent to that of a double no-foam latte. Individuals both inside the company and out questioned the value of the actual training that took place during those 3 hours. However, we think immeasurable *learning* resulted from the exercise. Starbucks employees relearned some crucial lessons. It wasn't so much how to *make* a perfect cup of coffee (something they probably already knew how to do), but rather how *important* it is to do so, in a world of growing competition and cost-consciousness. And Starbucks customers learned that the company about which they'd started to have a few doubts really was committed to being different from the rest.

Training Moves Careers

According to Alejandro Bustamante, president of Plantronics in Mexico, "The best person for almost any job we have is one we've grown and developed from within." That perspective has allowed his team to develop a simple but robust career plan that is fully integrated with the company's training process. Each of the plant's 140+ jobs has a prescribed list of competencies, each of which is mapped to the training course or courses necessary to develop it. Anyone who aspires to a new position can use the two huge binders displayed in the factory (and also on the facility's impressive intranet) to map the exact steps he or she must take to be prepared for any job.

"Our associates know that we prefer to promote from within, and that helps us keep the best people motivated to keep learning," Bustamante told me as we observed an assembly worker checking her career plan on one of the many intranet screens around the periphery of the massive plant. The Plamex *Plan de Carrera*, one of the most thorough yet easily administered career development systems we've seen, provides real clarity for employees' career growth. A design engineer in the company's research and development center told me, "I've been here for 11 years, and this is my fourth position. The *Plan de Carrera* has made it so easy for us to see what we need to do if we want to develop in the company. We still have to do the work, but the plan lays it all out for us. That's one reason I'm never leaving!"

The company provides the training, either internally or through an outside source. When a particular position becomes available, those who have completed the required courses comprise the pool of candidates considered. As a result, the company fills up to 60 percent of its position vacancies from within.

A man who carries a cat home by the tail learns ten times as much as one who only watches.

—Mark Twain, on distance learning

Beyond the Classroom and Webinar

Extensive technological developments—coupled with the desire for different training modalities on the part of a multigenerational workforce—have spurred the growth of distance learning and other nontraditional ways to deliver training. Although the *format* that companies use to deliver training is a significant consideration, it's *far less* important than *what* people learn—whether they're sitting in a classroom, standing at a functioning machine, listening to a podcast, or attending a webinar. Still, because of the variance in adult learning styles, the organizations that have the most to show for their training efforts are going well beyond didactic delivery styles with bulleted PowerPoint slides.

San Antonio–based USAA has held the number one or two spot on *BusinessWeek*'s ranking of Customer Service Champions every year since the magazine began publishing the list in 2007. They consistently enjoy a customer retention rate of 97.8 percent.[3] We can't help but wonder if part of this success comes from the all-encompassing nature of the company's training.

Not only are USAA's customer service representatives trained thoroughly on the technical aspects of their jobs, but they also learn what it's like to be a USAA customer, many of whom are active-duty members of the military, serving in war zones and other far-off places, and their families. In a typical scenario, reps dine on MREs (meals ready-to-eat), don Kevlar vests and flak helmets, and receive real deployment letters with fictitious names to help them better comprehend the realities of their customers' lives.

Quicken Loans has made great strides and had lots of fun with its "Quicken's Got Talent" program, named for the TV talent show *America's Got Talent*. As a way to share the best of what mortgage bankers are doing and develop their employees' phone skills, the contest allows bankers and their leaders to submit recorded customer calls to be considered for the competition. The contest progresses in steps and can culminate in big cash prizes. The fun and prizes motivate people to participate, but the real value has been the 400-plus recorded calls in the "Call Clip Library"—a sort of hit parade that bankers can access online to learn what works best when talking with current and potential clients. More than 69,000 playbacks have been recorded through the company's learning management system since the game's inception.[4]

An Intelligent Learning Process

The Contented Cow companies are deadly serious about the issue of training, with considerations that extend well beyond the amount of money they spend doing it, the impressiveness of their learning facilities, and the breadth of course offerings. What also makes them special is that despite the success they've enjoyed or how big they may have gotten, they have not lost sight of one of the most fundamental precepts in the whole workplace arena: that the person who started work for them this morning is as close to a "model employee" as they're ever going to get. And unlike so many others who no doubt recognize the same thing, they actively (fanatically might be a better word for it) *do* something about it.

Although we have cited how orientations (or onboarding) are an opportunity for employers to establish open, two-way communication with new hires from the outset, we cannot overemphasize the fact that orientations are primarily for training. Like many companies, Disney requires every single employee to attend a comprehensive new employee orientation, aka Disney Traditions. But the similarity between Disney and other companies ends there. Disney's focus is not so much on telling people where to find the paper clips, having them fill out forms until their fingers ache, or introducing them to dozens of new people who will likely be forgotten by lunchtime. Instead, they make sure to carefully and methodically introduce each new "cast member" to the company's traditions, philosophies, and a very different way of life—the Disney way.

Visibility Matters

Organizations too often send people to training without first securing leadership buy-in. Like it or not, people want to know that the training course they're taking their time to sit through is as important to senior management as it is supposed to be to them. This often requires senior management to ride along with them—not in their own condensed mini-versions, but alongside everyone else. There should be no executive parking spaces when it comes to training. Managers must participate enthusiastically and, more important, be able to demonstrate the skills they expect everyone else to learn. If nothing else, faithful adoption of this one suggestion would make the bozos who appear on CBS's *Undercover Boss* show seem a lot more competent.

When conducting leadership training for clients, we observe noticeable differences between groups that are "sent" to training without their bosses' participation versus groups where the boss is a fellow learner.

One such event involved a series of training sessions we delivered for a southeastern U.S. electrical utility. The training was conducted in a rural training facility about 100 miles from the company's headquarters. The vice president who brought us in underwent the training along with all of his direct reports, and his presence and participation in the training wasn't lost on anybody. The other class members truly appreciated his willingness to be observed in a new situation—a vulnerable, untrained state.

A few months later, we returned to provide the same program for a different, more junior group. Although the VP had already completed the training (and, by all accounts, was exhibiting his new skills), he wanted to put his stamp of support on the program for this group—even though the event's timeframe wasn't particularly convenient for him. Despite having an important meeting at headquarters, he thought it was important enough for him to kick off the training session that he took a company helicopter from the main office to the training facility early that morning.

At 7:45 AM, the VP landed at a nearby small airport. He then drove over to kick off the training program by telling the assembled group of the benefits he had realized since taking the course. Afterward, he and a colleague got in a car and drove south to the budget meeting. He made a 200-mile round trip to deliver a 10-minute message. What the employees gleaned from seeing their vice president standing in front of them— knowing the effort it took for him to be there—was more impactful than anything either of us said that day. He had sent the message loud and clear: "This is important—so important that I went through it before you did. I'm using it, and now I want and expect you to do the same."

By contrast, we conducted several training sessions for a large midwestern manufacturer. Because of the conspicuous absence of any member of senior management throughout the entirety of this effort, we often heard the question, "If this is so important, where are they?" Months later, an informal survey of attendees indicated that only a few people were using the skills they had learned in the course. It's possible the senior officers didn't really need to be there for their personal benefit; however, as we've heard so many times before, perception is reality. To us, it's a little like the difference between parents who send their children to church versus the ones who *take* them there.

A Quick Self-Exam

Sadly, we seldom go to the trouble of ensuring that the training efforts we've paid for and attended have actually *taught* our people anything. This is precisely why you should ask the following questions with respect to your organization's training efforts:

1. With respect to job skills training, have you established—and do you in fact train—to *minimum proficiency standards?*

2. How must *trainees demonstrate proficiency*, both on an initial and recurring basis? We're not just talking about skills training, either. (And while we're on the subject, why is it that no one ever flunks a corporate training program? Are both trainers and students *really* that good? Or do we just tend to let everyone "pass," regardless of performance?)

3. What *follow-up measures* do you have in place to ensure that people have actually *learned* something from a training effort and that they intend to use it in the future?

   One of our clients uses a simple but effective means to work on this one. After a training class (which she and her entire senior management team have usually attended first), her people receive an e-mail that asks them to describe for her in writing not only what they've learned but how they intend to put it to use:

Dear _____:

You have just completed a two-day XYZ Skills Workshop sponsored by our company. My hope is that the workshop was a success and that you are coming away armed with new skills that you can put to use.

My purpose in writing is to reinforce the expectation that you *do*, in fact, put the acquired skills and methods to use. Put simply, you and your fellow participants received this developmental opportunity because we believe that it will lead to more productive and satisfied managers and work units.

Within the next week, I would like for you to provide me a brief written summary detailing:

- What you learned
- How you intend to apply it in the course of your everyday job
- What I (or other members of our management team) can do to support you in this
- How, when, and by what means you plan to measure the relative success of these efforts

Sincerely,

Mary Q. Manager

4. *Who pays for the training?* Some might argue that it doesn't matter, as it all comes out of the same wallet anyhow—to which we reply, "Au contraire, seminar breath." If a training offering arrives as a gift of the training department or somebody else's cost center, it's not viewed with nearly the same seriousness as it would be if each department or work group were required to fund it themselves. Better yet, why not require each employee to personally budget (and account for) their *own* development expense?

5. Finally, and perhaps most important, *what are your training priorities?* Sounds like a stupid question, but most organizations don't have a clue. Instead, they approach the subject like a family of four in a Chinese restaurant: let's have one from column A, one from column B, and so on. And just like the Chinese meal, people eat what they like and don't eat what they don't want when the food shows up. The problem with this haphazard approach is that it virtually guarantees you'll spend more than you should, and you'll never get full—or, in business terms, reach the critical mass that is so essential to getting some return on that investment. If, for example, customer service training for frontline employees is a priority, then every single customer-facing employee ought to get it—no exceptions and no hall passes. If leadership training is a priority, then every single

leader ought to get it—no exceptions there, either! Think about it: How would you like to get on an airplane knowing that the captain and first officer had simply opted out of their emergency cockpit procedures class?

The process of establishing a cogent strategy for your training efforts yields some other benefits as well. For one thing, you'll inevitably consider more carefully the sequencing of training activities. You'll be forced to answer questions such as "Why don't we provide some leadership training for people *before* they move into a management position rather than having them practice on their new charges?"

Chapter Summary

Training is most assuredly a vital part of the enabling process and a factor that can (and should) be exploited as a key source of competitive advantage. Fully 90 percent of the $40 billion or so spent annually on training is being spent by only 0.5 percent of all U.S. companies, with much of that being wasted. You therefore *must* treat training as something other than a luxury by:

1. Linking it tightly to your business strategy
2. Knowing how to organize and deliver it
3. Setting clear return on investment expectations (individual as well as organizational)

Best Practices:
1. Training as part of the career plan at Plamex
2. Customer service "immersion" training at USAA
3. "Quicken's Got Talent"
4. New employee orientation at Disney

Enabled Employees Are Tooled

Tool(ed): To equip with the means for production.

The people who are doing the work are the moving force behind the Macintosh. My job is to create a space for them, to clear out the rest of the organization and keep it at bay.

—Steve Jobs

Tools, Not Rules

Organizations don't become Contented Cows purely on the strength of their human resources practices or their managers' leadership skills. All of the policies, methods, systems, habits, and procedures that comprise your organization's operating environment work together to have a positive or negative impact on your workforce and its members' willingness to part with that most precious commodity: their own discretionary effort.

It does no good to hire talented people who fit well within the organization, get them all fired up about the voyage, equip them with a capable leader, and train the stew out of them, if one or more forces within your organization's system are going to prevent them from performing.

One of the biggest motivators is being able to see progress made at the end of each shift or day. Most of us want to work in an environment where we can do our very best work, and it makes us crazy when dumb (or poorly executed) leadership actions or systemic obstacles keep that from happening.

Training people well and then standing in their way is analogous to spending a half million dollars to build a NASCAR race car, another half million to get a backup car, hiring a top-name driver and pit crew, paying for months of practice—and then sending your crew chief out to put a governor on the engine 30 minutes before the race. While none of us would knowingly do something this stupid, we somehow manage to pull it off on a fairly regular basis. We do it by providing incentives that encourage people to do exactly what we *don't* want, establishing policies that are misguided at best, utilizing systems that treat intelligent people like they're complete morons, and developing cultures that ensure that no mistake goes unpunished.

> *Ninety percent of what we call "management" consists of making it difficult for people to get things done.*
>
> —Peter Drucker

Be Careful What You Incent; You'll Likely Get It!

At the risk of offending some of our friends in the compensation profession, we're going to say that most pay systems suck a big egg. They not only fail to motivate people to do their best; they actually induce them to do a *poor* job in many cases.

Perhaps the most obvious example is the system of paying someone based on how long they take to complete a task—a notion that is fundamentally bankrupt in nearly every case (and could have the same effect on your fortunes). Anybody with a pulse can figure out pretty quickly what they need to do to make more money under such a time-based scheme, and it's not in your customers' or stockholders' interest for them to do it. So why in the world do we pay people that way? Some would have you believe that it is required by law, but that's not true. Companies like Worthington Industries and Chaparral Steel have known this for a long time, as their employees are all salaried.

You must be especially careful about what you incent people to do, because that is exactly what they're *going* to do. Sears realized this in the early 1990s, when, as the result of a new pay plan for its automotive service people, they wound up with a public relations nightmare when the company was accused of systematically defrauding car repair customers by making unneeded repairs.[1]

Conversely, Cleveland-based manufacturer of electric motors Lincoln Electric has enjoyed immense success over its 100-plus-year history. This is due in part to its unique piecework pay system, which incents employees to do exactly what they're supposed to do *and* earn above-average compensation in the process. In a book about the company titled *Spark*, author Frank Koller explains, "Lincoln Electric has always operated under the assumption that an energetic pursuit of corporate profits is not inhibited by an equally determined commitment to raise the fortunes of its employees; in fact, the two are interdependent."[2] This idea seems to be working pretty well for Lincoln Electric, which scored an average annual growth rate of 19 percent during the tough Wall Street years of 2005 to 2009, provided its investors a yearly return on investment of 16 percent during those years, and grabbed the number one global market share in the industry.

While we're on the topic of broken systems, let's talk about sick days, this rather curious system, based on a traditional model and some rather convoluted logic. Under most plans, employees (the lucky ones) are given a finite number of days during which they're permitted to call in sick and still be paid. Although we've made some progress toward more sensible solutions to the need for time off in the past decade, we're amazed at how widespread the old practice remains. The intent of such plans is obvious, but given the way most of them are designed, people feel compelled to use up their allotment of days each year—regardless of whether or not they actually become ill.

The way we choose to handle paid time off is a little bit like the different approaches a bank or other financial institution could take in protecting its customers against overdrafts. One approach would be for the institution to simply "stake" each customer to an additional $1,000 each year—using real money, deposited by the bank into the customer's account, with the caveat that the money should be used only to protect against overdrafts. (We've got a pretty good idea how this scenario would play out.)

Alternatively, they could take a different approach and tell credit-worthy customers that they will temporarily "cover" account overdrafts (within reason)—and, as my own banker put it, "If you abuse the privilege or use it too often, we will have to revisit the relationship, or perhaps terminate it altogether."

A body of evidence is beginning to develop suggesting that companies that take this latter approach with the issue of sick days are experiencing significantly fewer unscheduled absences. In some cases, they've averaged unscheduled absence rates of less than 1 percent of scheduled workdays versus a mean of around 1.6 percent for all employers.

It's not our intention to tell you how you should allot time off; rather, we encourage you to evaluate whether or not your current system prompts the behavior you'd like to see from employees. Instead of allocating x number of days (or even hours) for sick leave, family leave, so-called personal leave, and vacation—with complicated formulas for disbursing and accounting for each—why not consider a simpler approach? Some of the more sensible plans deposit time into a PTO (paid time off) bank and let people use the time as they see fit. Employers budget for it, and managers work it into their resource planning. In some cases, employees can cash in unused time or carry it forward to subsequent years. Better yet—although this might be too far a leap for many—truly treat your employees like fully responsible adults, as Bazaarvoice and Netflix do, and throw out your time-off policy altogether (see Chapter 9).

Help Not Hinder

Contented Cows go to elaborate lengths to develop and implement not only policies but procedures and support systems designed to make heroes (not scapegoats) out of their employees, especially those who serve on the front line.

Established in 1954 in Cincinnati, LaRosa's Pizzeria is a regional chain of full-service Italian restaurants that offers dine-in, carryout, and delivery from 65 stores in Ohio, Kentucky, and Indiana. On a visit to a LaRosa's, you're as likely to see a family celebrating a special occasion as you are a mom taking a night off from the kitchen with her kids or a Little League team enjoying a victory dinner. What you're not likely to *see*, although they're in full operation in the background, are lean manufacturing processes. Despite the fact that this approach is more often used in the huge national high-end chains than in smaller, family-oriented restaurants, LaRosa's has embraced it. Based on a philosophy that enhances customer value with more targeted work that minimizes waste, the company has improved the experience for the customer *and* the team member, while saving money and increasing margin.

"We used to have, like, six ice scoops in some stores," LaRosa's executive director of HR Steve Browne told us. "You only need *one*. But it would get lost, so we'd order another one. Now, there's a designated place for the ice scoop, and people are trained on that, and every time you need it, guess what—it's there! Simple things like that [are what make a difference]." And it's more. Rather than prepping some food items in advance, a process that was *thought* to increase efficiency, LaRosa's has reengineered the process with a just-in-time flavor. They don't lose a second from order to serving and manage to enhance quality and minimize waste at the same time. They accurately match labor supply with demand at every hour of the day so that they waste neither their customers' nor their team members' time. Since "going lean," LaRosa's has increased gross margin, brought labor cost down from 35 percent to 25 percent, and improved employee satisfaction scores substantially. And their customer service consistently remains in the 99th percentile on a comparable industry-wide basis.

Likewise, our friends at the Plantronics headset factory in Tijuana have capitalized on the power of *process* to vastly improve their ability to respond to customers' needs. They are simplifying workers' jobs and allowing them to focus on more productive and fulfilling tasks, rather than on the minutiae that tends to grind people down. The company's challenge was to reflect its corporate vision of "Simply Smarter Communication," with "Simply Smarter Manufacturing." Relying on their considerable brainpower alone (not PhDs from MIT or Stanford), they annihilated the complexity inherent in a system that produces more than 16,000 different products using 50,000 raw materials and ushered in a process that allows them to change their product line up to 30 times a day with ease and produce from 1 to 10,000 units of any given item. There was a time when it took up to six weeks to fill special orders. Today, they can fill virtually all orders, special or routine, in 48 hours. And the scrap rate is perhaps the lowest in the industry, plummeting to 0.14 percent of material *cost*, against an industry standard of 1.0 percent of *sales price*.

A Tale of Two Brands

It was the best of service; it was the worst of service. Well, not really the worst, but with this heading, I couldn't resist.

Not long after Amazon introduced its third-generation Kindle e-reader, my business partner, the coauthor of this book, gave me one of the new gadgets as a gift—thereby telling the younger of us that I really needed to transition my reading platform to something a little less fifteenth century.

Although it surprised me (but not him) a little, I was an instant convert. And so I was positively disconsolate when the reader stopped working several months later, on the first day of a three-week-long international trip.

As soon as I discovered the problem, during a layover at New York's JFK Airport, I logged into my Amazon account from my laptop, clicked "Support," and typed in my mobile number. My phone rang almost immediately. Yep—*they* called *me!* I didn't have to look up a number, dial it, navigate through an infernal scheme of menus, listen to hold music, and plead for a real human. One called *me!*

By virtue of my having logged into my account before I requested the call, the Amazon rep knew everything I wanted her to know (and probably more). She didn't ask me for my account number *once*, let alone *twice*. She grieved in sympathy with me (momentarily) over the device's demise, told me that it was irreparable by telephone troubleshooting, and without even *suggesting* that I might have done something myself to damage it, said she'd "send me a replacement by 2nd Day Air."

"I hate to sound ungrateful," I said sheepishly, "because I really do appreciate the offer, but I'm getting on a transatlantic flight in two hours and I'll be kind of a moving target for the next three weeks. My wife, however, will be home until tomorrow afternoon, and then she's flying over to meet me."

"Then I'll just send it overnight!" the rep countered, as though *I* were doing *her* a favor. "Your wife will have it by 10:30 in the morning. Will that work?"

Of *course* it would work! And it did. Two days later, I met my wife in the Rome airport. She'd been kind enough to load the replacement

Kindle with my content before leaving home (international downloads are pricey!) and pack it in her luggage. She and the Amazon rep—enabled by the company's policies, systems, and customer philosophy—allowed me to have an almost limitless supply of reading material on the combination vacation and business trip. Bravo, Amazon!

Unfortunately, I can't say the same for Panasonic. While on the trip, I took lots of pictures with my new Panasonic Lumix digital camera—a great camera that takes terrific pictures. But I was surprised when, shortly before my trip, the camera arrived without the software disc described in the manual—the piece of equipment that lets the camera communicate with a computer. Not a big deal, but an annoyance, especially if you want to do any of the cool things designed into the software, like stitching together panoramic shots, or making it appear as though you visited exotic places that you never actually saw.

Packing CDs in a box, I thought, is so first decade. Surely it's a download these days, and they just haven't updated the manual. That explains the empty slot in the box, obviously designed to hold a compact disc.

Wrong. After I got home, I went to Panasonic's website but got no help there. I then picked up the phone to give them a call. After a long wait, during which I was reminded ad nauseam of the importance of my call to them (if it's that important, then call *me*, like Amazon did), customer service sent me to tech support, which sent me back to customer service, where a snippy woman who didn't believe my story of the missing software gave me the number for the parts department, like I was calling a Honda dealer or something. (I'm not making this up.)

Twenty minutes later, someone from parts answered. They wanted my name, phone number, e-mail address, account number (again), and—get this—the serial number of the item I was calling about—before they'd entertain any questions.

I asked how I could download the software. I learned that I couldn't; that they'd have to send me a CD. Oh, please do. I learned that it would cost me $15. An argument ensued, and I surrendered the credit card number to cut my time losses.

Ten days later, I hadn't yet received the CD. However, I did get a paper receipt in the mail from Panasonic, documenting my $23 (including shipping) purchase. Someone actually cut down a tree, refined its pulp into paper, printed a receipt, stuck it in an envelope, put it in a truck, took it to the post office, transferred it to a jet, put it on yet another truck, then a van, and then a nice man who works for an inefficient quasi-governmental agency walked it to my house.

Five days after that, the CD turned up on my front doorstep.

Both Amazon and Panasonic have now burned their respective brands into my psyche. I associate Amazon with terms like *pathfinder, state-of-the-art service, friendly, impressive*, and *exceeds customer expectations*.

Panasonic now means something different to me, and it's not very impressive.

What does this have to do with compelling your employees to expend their discretionary effort? In short, everything. Product and service brand extend to workplace brand. I wonder (not really) which company's getting the best candidates turning up on its front doorstep and which of the service reps I spoke to went home at day's end more fulfilled.

The Meaning of Mistakes

3M is a Contented Cow that knows a thing or two about making mistakes. With 50,000 different products on the market and an internal requirement that 30 percent of each year's sales must come from products less than four years old, they've undoubtedly experienced lots of missteps along the way. They realize—perhaps better than most—that the relentless pursuit of innovation is anything but a straight path.

Former 3M president William L. McKnight explained the company's approach in a paper titled "Philosophy of Management" published in 1941:

> *[If the] men and women to whom we delegate authority and responsibility are good people, [they] are going to want to do their jobs in their own way . . . Mistakes will be made, but if a person is essentially right, the mistakes he or she makes are not as serious in the long run as the mistakes management will make if it is dictatorial and undertakes to tell those under its authority exactly how they must do their job. Management that is destructively critical when mistakes are made kills initiative, and it is essential that we have people with initiative if we are to continue to grow.[3]*

We must be careful to find the right balance between having the procedures, standards, and routinization that are necessary to a high-performing organization and avoiding the impediments that frustrate ideas and best effort.

The hustlinest team makes the most mistakes.
> —John Wooden, legendary UCLA basketball coach

Mistakes Must Absolutely, Positively Not Go Unpunished

We said early on that we're not holding the Contented Cows out as models of perfection and that occasionally, they, too step in some "cow chips." However, they're usually very fleet of foot at both recognizing and learning from these errors.

For instance, throughout much of the 1980s, the nature and characteristics of the average package tendered to FedEx changed. Packages became smaller and lighter in weight, grew in number, and contained vital correspondence rather than goods and materials. The company responded beautifully with the successful marketing of the now ubiquitous FedEx Letter. However, some new and different operating problems accompanied the precipitous growth in letter volume.

One of the more vexing problems resulted from the size and dimensions of the Overnight Letter envelope (as it was then known), and the envelope's propensity for getting lost in the back of the company's delivery vans. As they picked up packages throughout the day, couriers would return to the van, put the freight in the back, and drive off to their next stop. Over the course of the afternoon, these loose packages—particularly, the Overnight Letter envelopes—had a nasty habit of sliding around and finding their way into small crevices in the cargo section. This of course made them invisible to the courier who unloaded the truck at the end of the day.

The net result was that the overlooked letter(s) remained in the van overnight (or perhaps several nights) before someone discovered them— meaning that countless customers *weren't* getting what they had paid for. At the time, the company had more than 30,000 couriers and carried approximately a million packages per night, roughly half of which were Overnight Letters. It doesn't take a rocket scientist to figure out the huge potential magnitude of the problem—and that a lot of packages were practically begging to be misplaced on any given day!

Despite all the things they've done well over the years, FedEx management uncharacteristically reacted in a shortsighted manner. (And since one of us was one of those managers, we're pointing the finger at ourselves as much as anyone else.) We took the position that these overlooked packages were obviously the result of a careless or uncommitted workforce. Therefore, we decided to impose formal, written disciplinary action in any (and every) situation where an employee overlooked a package. The warning letters soon began to pile up by the hundreds, giving birth to new expressions ("Leave a letter, get a letter"), and over time, these reprimands actually became something of a status symbol. In the eyes of many couriers, you were nobody unless you had at least one written warning.

But it was no laughing matter, because a lot of otherwise good employees lost their jobs due to an accumulation of warning letters in the process. (FedEx believed in the three strikes and you're out approach). Moreover, the overlooked package problem didn't get better; it got worse! Some couriers may or may not have been lazy, but they certainly weren't stupid. With foreknowledge of exactly what would happen if they ever did discover an overlooked package in the back of their van, many took direct measures to ensure that no such package was ever discovered. It wasn't until the company backed off the "every mistake will be punished" approach and began actively soliciting courier ideas that we began to solve this problem.

"Good Faith" Mistakes versus Errors of the Heart

Our research and experience suggest that the Contented Cows (including FedEx) have done a better than average job of reducing the level of fear within their organizations. Somewhat consistent with the views espoused by former Intel CEO Andy Grove, they've focused not on the fairly healthy fear of survival, but the paralyzing fear that stems from the capricious exercise of power.

Contented Cow companies reduce some of this unnecessary fear by establishing systemic measures that minimize the possibility of arbitrary or capricious treatment; by taking a longer view of the expected length of the employment relationship; and by permitting (and even encouraging) their people to actively experiment and make some mistakes.

They make a broad distinction, however, between the types of mistakes that busy people are inclined to make when they're really leaning forward and doing their level best to produce, versus the errors of the heart in which a person knowingly violates one of the organization's core precepts. And they don't suffer "sinners" very well in the latter cases.

Chapter Summary

1. Tooling is the process of ridding your organization of success inhibitors, those things that keep people from either doing the right things or doing things right. Some examples:

   o Policies that are antiquated or just plain dumb

   o Practices that frustrate rather than support personal effort

   o Systems (e.g., pay, sick days) that encourage or even reward people for doing the wrong things

   o Failed communication methods that guarantee that nobody understands anything

2. Processes can make all the difference between a satisfied employee serving both the customer and the organization and a frustrated one serving neither.

3. You must discern between good faith mistakes and "errors of the heart."

Better Practices:

1. Salaried workforces at Worthington Industries and Chaparral Steel

2. Lincoln Electric's "piecework pay system"

3. Lean manufacturing processes at LaRosa's Pizzeria

4. Redesign of manufacturing processes at Plantronics, for lightning-fast customer responsiveness

5. "Don't call us—we'll call *you!*" customer service system at Amazon

CHAPTER 13

Enabled Employees
Are Trusted

*Few things can help an individual more than to place responsibility on
him, and to let him know that you trust him.*

—Booker T. Washington

In Chapter 6, we wrote of what we called a "truth recession" that both
predated and accompanied the 2007–2009 worldwide financial recession. It seems accurate to say that the workforce's trust in their management has sustained damage that is at worst irreparable and at best will
require a long rehabilitation. No less significant in the way that institutions function is the degree of trust that travels in the other direction—
the trust that organizations vest in their people.

Think about it: in their private lives, your employees (and ours) are
heads of families, civic leaders, military reserve officers, mortgage hold-
ers, and a host of other things. They somehow manage to feed themselves
and their families every day, pay their bills on time, stay out of jail, and
behave normally by most standards. In short, they tend to be rather competent individuals who clearly understand the difference between right
and wrong.

Why is it, then, that these people face a continual barrage of not so subtle signs of our mistrust in them when they come to work? We seem to find new ways every day to treat them like children, or worse. If you disagree, consider this: if you offered to pay a neighbor's teenager to pick up some groceries for you at the store, which of the following—if any— would you do when they returned with the groceries:

- Ask to see their time card, signed by a parent or supervisor.
- Check their odometer readings and each item's price tag.
- Read them your eight-page policy on grocery purchases.
- March them through a metal detector at your front door.
- Double count your change.
- Demand a receipt.

We didn't think so. Now, if you're not going to require such an accounting from the kid down the street, why would you think of doing so with someone who has presumably passed your panel interview process, had their employment and criminal references checked, completed a personality profile, and successfully peed in a bottle? After all, this is someone you have an opportunity to observe working for 8 hours a day.

Trust, integrity, call it what you will, but whether it's as a customer, supplier, or employee, it is one of the key factors that differentiates the Contented Cows from the also-rans. What really distinguishes trusting from distrusting relationships—and there is no middle ground—is the ability of those involved to make a leap of faith. In short, they believe that each party is interested in and committed to the other's welfare and that neither will act without first considering the action's impact on the other.

> We've had an extraordinary year, despite major inflation of raw materials, and I can say that the single biggest contributor has been an increase in trust. We now move through enormously complex decisions at breakneck speed.
>
> —Al Carey, CEO, Frito-Lay[1]

Nordstrom Trust—As Simple as It Gets

Seattle-based department store Nordstrom has become synonymous with legendary customer service. Something must be working, because in a cutthroat industry with competitors entering (and exiting) the market almost every day, this company doubled sales between 2002 and 2011 (arguably some of the bleakest years in U.S. retail history). This gave it the highest revenue growth of any department store in the country.[2] Patrons keep coming because what everybody says about Nordstrom is true: they have outstanding customer service *and* great merchandise.

We get one clue as to how they're able to get their 52,000 employees to render such outstanding service via the simple "Welcome Card" that every new Nordstrom employee receives on his or her first day:

Welcome to Nordstrom

We're glad to have you with our company.

Our number one goal is to provide outstanding customer service.

Set both your personal and professional goals high. We have great confidence in your ability to achieve them.

Nordstrom rules:

1. Use your good judgment in all situations.

2. Please feel free to ask your department manager, store manager, or division general manager any question at any time.

For years, this card was proudly called the "Nordstrom Employee Handbook" and was described as such in the first edition of this book. In the meantime, apparently someone with a law degree got ahold of it and decided that every employee should still receive it—since it is, indeed, the way the company works. However, it now accompanies a real book, complete with rules and regulations. We would respectfully suggest that they should have left well enough alone.

Nevertheless, unlike so many of the rest of us, Nordstrom apparently believes they made the right choice at the outset—by hiring adults with some modicum of good sense and judgment. The simplicity of the two rules—which causes them to treat their people as mature, competent professionals—is simply an extension of that faith.

We've found that people tend to base trust as much on the personal (i.e., manager-employee) relationship as on the organization's policies and practices. This seems clear from the fact that one can still find pockets of high morale and productivity, even in organizations where some very bad things are going on. It may be analogous to the underpinnings of motivation long understood and taught by the military—chiefly, the notion that when push comes to shove, people don't fight for the flag or Mom or apple pie. Instead, they fight for the guy standing next to them. Their trust is based not on symbols or feelings but reality.

Rethinking the Break Room

As with so many other things, we demonstrate trust in small, seemingly infinitesimal ways. SAS Institute, for instance, apparently believes that "well-fed cows give better milk." Every floor of each of the 18 buildings on its sprawling Cary, North Carolina, campus has a well-stocked break room with a veritable cornucopia of stuff to eat and drink—"everything from crackers to M&M's," according to one employee—all of which the company pays for. There's nothing to stop someone from shoving three boxes of Cracker Jack in their bag and schlepping them home for those nights when they've got the munchies. Well, maybe there is—the fact that they're trusted *not* to.

Let's not be naive. There are absolutely some untrustworthy characters out there and a few others who just don't get it. In a nutshell, our advice is simple. Get rid of them, *now*, or whenever and wherever they pop up. We also realize that we live in a post–Oklahoma City, post-9/11 world that has sadly become nearly obsessed with security. We're not talking about sensible measures that everyone must take to ensure that our assets, human and otherwise, remain safe. We're talking about the small proportion of people who somehow manage to find their way inside organizations but who don't have the organization's interests at heart. But trust *us* on this one: the answer to this is *not* to try to bring these people into line by enacting dumb policies and other measures. This does little more than frustrate the efforts of hundreds of capable, hardworking, honest people who are simply trying to get their work done—and it just won't work. The only thing you're going to get from spending precious time and energy building bigger and better mousetraps is smarter mice. Or as FedEx founder Fred Smith is fond of saying, "We're not going to lower the river—we can only raise the bridge."

Consider as well that enacting such measures can make them self-fulfilling prophecies, due to the crystal clear message they send to every affected person: "We really don't *expect* you to get it right." For that reason alone, they probably won't. It's really not unlike the experience so many companies have had with their quality efforts. The moment they install QC inspectors, quality goes down the tube as people begin to relax, falsely secure in the hope that someone else will now catch all their errors.

HP's David Packard recounted such an example from his work at General Electric in Schenectady in the 1930s:

> *The company was making a big thing of plant security. GE was especially zealous about guarding its tool and parts bins to make sure employees didn't steal anything. Faced with this obvious display of distrust, many employees set out to prove it justified, walking off with tools or parts whenever they could. Eventually GE tools and parts were scattered all around town including the attic of the house in which a number of us were living. In fact, we had so much equipment up there that when we threw the switch, the lights on the entire street would dim.*[3]

In later years, Packard and HP cofounder Bill Hewlett took pains to ensure that their company learned from GE's mistakes by insisting that lab storerooms remain unlocked. Said Packard, "the open bins and storerooms were a symbol of trust, a trust that is central to the way HP does business."[4]

> *If you assign people heavy responsibilities, that implies confidence in them, and belief in their ability to deliver the goods. Such a move stimulates their desire to prove your faith is well-founded.*
>
> —Price Pritchett

Opening the Kimono

You can measure the degree to which an organization trusts people by the amount and nature of the information it chooses to share with them. We've all seen internal company intranets, and frankly, many of the ones

I've seen are hardly more useful than a tissue is for scraping ice off a windshield. Many contain indecipherable data throughout a system of unnavigable pages, and some are more internal marketing than anything else.

Plamexnet, the intranet used by Tijuana-based manufacturer Plamex, is different. I was amazed at the brilliantly organized plethora of information that's available to all Plamex associates via any of the dozens of screens placed conveniently around the plant. "Everyone can have access to everything," company president Alejandro Bustamante told me, and then demonstrated. "The only exceptions are patents, salaries, and anything restricted by Plantronics corporate." After being logged into the secure system—and without receiving further instructions—I was able to easily access Plamex's strategic plan and observe how the plant was performing against it. I could see sales, cost, scrap, and all sorts of other production data expressed with illustrative graphics and in crystal clear terms that anyone—even I—could understand. Anyone who wants to know what the big bosses talked about in the weekly staff meeting can easily access each meeting's minutes—right there for all to peruse.

Raise Discretionary Authority and Spending Limits

One of the first areas we'd suggest you look at is the amount of discretionary authority you vest in your employees, since it is woefully inadequate in virtually all cases. Get them involved in the hiring process—not as mere bystanders, but as decision makers. Better yet, put them *in charge* of it. Involve them in promotional decisions, especially those involving frontline management positions. Put them in charge of manpower scheduling. Permit them (no, *require* them) to be personally involved in and responsible for some spending decisions. Levi Strauss, for example, has been known to involve its forklift drivers in the purchasing of new forklift trucks.

At a minimum, afford your employees unquestioned authority to commit an amount of resource equivalent to at least one week's pay to improve their ability to do their jobs or to satisfy a customer. Managers (or team-based units) operating with their own cost center or profit and loss statements should have at least four to five times that much discretionary authority.

He'd Give You the Pants off His Legs

On his delightful blog (http://www.blogs.marriott.com/marriott-on-the-move/), Bill Marriott shared the unique story of a guest at the Marriott Residence Inn in Mississauga, a Toronto suburb. This gentleman had presented himself at the hotel's front desk one morning with a look of panic on his face. In his haste to make his trip, he had accidentally packed his wife's slacks instead of the dress pants he'd intended to wear to a meeting that was to take place very soon in the hotel. He was hoping there might be an extra pair in the hotel's lost and found or that someone could direct him to a store very nearby.

The lost and found yielded nothing, but one of the hotel's front desk associates, a man named Krasi, noticed that he and the guest happened to be about the same size and offered him the trousers he was wearing—thereby saving the day. Fortunately, Krasi had a spare pair of casual slacks that he could wear while his more formal trousers were on loan. As Marriott said, "While he didn't exactly give him the shirt off his back, he sure gave him the pants off his legs."

This incident clearly shows that Marriott trusts—encourages, really—its people to look for opportunities for service and make whatever decisions they deem necessary to serve their guests. There's no rule requiring associates to lend clothing—or anything else, for that matter—to guests. But, and this is perhaps more significant, there's no rule that prohibits it.

Powerlessness corrupts. Absolute powerlessness corrupts absolutely.
—Rosabeth Moss Kanter

Chapter Summary

1. Trust is the habit of letting go, *really* letting go, of a practice without which you will be doomed to an unacceptably slow pace. It is neither one-dimensional nor negotiable.
2. Do away with systemic signs of distrust (e.g., unnecessary policies, probation periods, time clocks, locked supply cabinets, etc.).
3. Dramatically increase levels of discretionary authority.

4. Remember that the aim is not to make people feel powerful but to keep them from feeling power*less*.

5. Deal swiftly (and harshly) with those who "break faith"—but do it individually.

Better Practices:

1. Plamex's highly useful and transparent intranet

2. SAS Institute's free snacks in the break room

3. Nordstrom's Welcome Card (formerly known as the Employee Handbook)

When the Contented Cows Come Home

Speculations on the Near Future

The Contented Cows . . . What Next?

As before, we've put a little pressure on the 12 Contented Cow companies (and a lot more on ourselves) by offering them as examples for others to follow. Their reputations are what they are, and we happen to think they're well deserved. Yet, one has to wonder just a little about whether they and their shareholders will continue to enjoy the advantages they've created. Will they keep living up to and redefining what it takes and means to be a Contented Cow? Or will they rest on their laurels while others pass them by? Only time will tell. Clearly, it's within their capability to do the former and within human or corporate nature to do the latter. The question is: Will they remain a breed apart? Does it mean enough to them?

Is it possible some of them have already become just a little too enam-ored of themselves or spend more time than they should reading their own press clippings? We wish we could be more certain.

The Path Ahead

Organizations must realize that just as they have choices, their employees (particularly the better, more skilled ones) do, too. The new rules of the game have been set, and now it's only a matter of time before everyone learns how to play, and play it to their advantage.

For example, employees will adjust to their newfound responsibility for their work, careers, and future, which is good, because it's about time. But those organizations that refuse to provide people with the information and tools they need to do their best work—and to make valid decisions about their future—will face real difficulty. Any parent who has watched a child go from the teen years to adulthood knows precisely how this goes. We must either continue to alter the nature of the partnership by putting it on an ever more adult-type footing or watch helplessly as they run off and leave *us*.

As predicted in the earlier version of this work, we have evolved to having at least four different classes of employees in the workplace. Each one has varying degrees of connectedness to the organization and totally different pay and benefit schemes. The determination of who winds up in what class of job, for how long, and under what conditions is made as often by the employee as it is by the organization. And to remove any doubt about it, that choice is made for selfish reasons. It's no longer analo-gous just to the world of professional sports, where players simultaneously engage in multiple sports—or at the very least, have become expert at leveraging their free agency. Nowadays, we see free agent contractors in health care, information technology, and even the military.

Just in timing, work process disaggregation, and the externalization of the workforce will remain with us. To the extent that we employ contrac-tors, temporary workers, or part-timers in core activities, we must find new ways of harnessing or positioning their effort as a distinct competi-tive advantage. Otherwise, everyone winds up working for Manpower, and things such as dedication and willingness to part with discretionary effort will go the way of loyalty.

No More Big Brooms or Silver Bullets

Managers have gotten somewhat of a break over the past several years in that the big brooms of downsizing and rightsizing have enabled them to gracefully disguise the firing of nonperformers and malcontents. We were able to push these individuals out the door with everybody else and do it with less commotion and unpleasantness than if it had happened on a case-by-case basis. But the big brooms are becoming silent. There aren't too many companies left with a need to undergo the kind of radical restructuring we've seen over the past decade.

Given the heightened importance of everyone on our payroll, we simply must do a much better job of facing up to performance issues. Appraisal and the whole performance improvement process remain of paramount importance. And let's face it: we've done a miserable job with this in the past. The Deming crowd and a lot of HR professionals who have grown weary of the fight would have us believe that we should just do away with the process. But with all due respect, they're wrong. It's an issue far too important to simply shrug our shoulders and run away from. We've got to figure it out—sooner rather than later.

Pat Riley, president of the Miami Heat NBA franchise dealt with the subject head on in his book *The Winner Within*. According to Riley, "Avoiding the solution of a tough, miserable problem is not discretion. It's cowardice. And it's robbery. Because as long as a serious problem goes unsolved, no team, no person can exploit its full potential. Any coach who doesn't kick the complacent ass on his team will wind up kicking his own before long."[1]

Keeping Them Fired Up and in the Game

Managers will have to work harder than ever to make their organizations attractive places to work. If we can't—or won't—offer security, we must offer real challenge and lots of freedom to pursue it. The good news is that people really *do* thrive on challenge and achievement—both the team's and their own. But it's up to us to invent the game, sell it, explain the rules, and erect the scoreboard.

We applaud the many corporations that have gone to great lengths to get their people feeling like owners. That's what it's all about. Quite a few have even pursued a path of actually *making* them owners, via stock options, grants, and the like. And that's even better. But despite all the communication methods at our disposal, few have let their employees know about them effectively, and even fewer have bothered to clearly articulate anything about the vagaries of the market and the occasional effects this little thing called gravity has on it. Most of us have already experienced firsthand the diminishing motivational return on investment one gets from underwater stock options. So what makes us think our people will feel any different?

Although we needn't build an entire town as Milton Hershey did, we must resolve the issue of benefits, particularly health care. As the Committee for Economic Development's Frank Doyle pointed out, neither we nor our workers can well afford the incongruity between having a more flexible workforce and our antiquated benefit structures.[2]

Moreover, in the case of health care benefits in particular, we must be mindful of the fact that we now have an entire generation of baby boomers starting to fall apart at an ever-increasing rate. All of this is occurring at a time when more and more of them don't have health coverage. Whether those people are real employees in the traditional sense, contract workers, or something else is immaterial. As Robert Owen figured out, if they're sick, hurt, or busted up—they can't work!

So What About You?

In as compelling a way as we know how, we've tried to illustrate the distinct and valuable advantages of treating people right. If nothing else, maybe what we've done is confirm for your head what your heart has known all along. The 12 companies we chose to profile in the Contented Cow comparison ended up with a $70 billion annual wealth advantage for shareholders. How much more incentive do you really need?

We fervently hope that some of the facts or ideas we've shared will become a cause for action. But if you intend to change some of your managerial behaviors, or perhaps your outlook or assumptions—even in a small way—you must do it with a sense of urgency. Don't wait, because time is not your friend. Yet you must also be deliberate. You can start by taking a no-nonsense, clear-eyed look at the way you personally are operating now—no copping out or scapegoating. To those who would say, "But geez,

I can't really do some of these things until my boss plows the way, or our system just won't let me . . ."—we say, *"Bull!" Find* a way! Go ahead without them! The truth is you can start making a difference in your company right now, without anyone's help or permission.

And just what is your company or business, anyhow? You know as well as we do it's not the name over the door. It is not a brand, a logo, or nameplate. It isn't even the products you make or services you sell. Nor is it a ticker symbol, a bank account, or a piece of paper your attorney filed in Delaware long ago.

Instead, it's you—because as our friend Jeb Blount pointed out in his book of the same name: *People Follow You*. And it's the people who will (or won't) show up for work tomorrow morning and the attitude they bring with them when they pass through the front door. It's their ideas, their sweat, their emotions, their energy . . . their expectations of and faith in you. It's both what they are, and what they can become.

It's people who individually and collectively, but not always consciously, decide whether to:

- Walk with a spring in their step or to shuffle their feet.
- Smile at customers even when they're having a bad day themselves.
- Use the tools you've provided with purpose and conviction, or take them home and put them in the attic.
- Show up early and stay late, or hit the snooze button, roll over, and call in sick.
- Walk through fire for you, or merely hang on well enough to avoid getting fired by you.
- Say "I can help," as opposed to "That's not my job."
- Find a way to do it better, faster, and cheaper, or simply settle for "good enough."
- Make something great happen here, or instead vote with their feet.

Again, it's a matter of choice . . . yours and then theirs. Good luck and Godspeed!

NOTES

Chapter 1   Just the Facts

1. "Levi's: As Ye Sew, so Shall Ye Reap," *Fortune*, May 12, 1997, 106.
2. Cliff Hanley, *History of Scotland* (New York: Gallery Books, 1986), 98.

Chapter 2   Cows with Attitude

1. Roosevelt Thomas, *Beyond Race and Gender* (New York: AMACOM, 1991), 14.
2. J. Albright, "Improving the Welfare of Dairy Cows Through Management," *Business and Management* (1982).
3. Jack Stack, *The Great Game of Business* (New York: Doubleday, 1992), 9.
4. Dennis Organ, *Business Horizons*, May–June 1995.
5. National Institute on Aging Study, 1973.
6. Organ, op. cit.
7. Albright, op. cit.
8. Jimmy Johnson, *Turning the Thing Around* (New York: Hyperion, 1993), 180.
9. "Money, Talent, and the Devil By the Tail: J. Willard Marriott," *Management Review*, January 1985.
10. Frederick F. Reicheld, *The Loyalty Effect* (Boston: Harvard Business School Press, 1996), 105

Chapter 3   The "Vision Thing": Passengers or Crew

1. Frederick W. Smith, speech at Rhodes College, February 25, 1988.
2. "Success," May 1994, 64.
3. Jan Carlzon, *Moments of Truth* (Cambridge, MA: Ballinger, 1987), 3.
4. Jack Stack, *The Great Game of Business* (New York: Doubleday, 1992), 57.

Chapter 4   The Path to Commitment

1. Francis J. Aguilar and Arvind Bhambri, Johnson & Johnson, Harvard Business School Case #384-053, 4.
2. Noel Tichy and Stratford Sherman, *Control Your Destiny or Someone Else Will* (New York: Bantam, 1993), 245–246.
3. Kevin and Jackie Freiberg, *NUTS!* (Austin, TX: Bard, 1996), 49.
4. Peter Lynch, *Beating the Street* (New York: Simon & Schuster, 1993), 27.
5. David Packard, *The HP Way* (New York: HarperBusiness, 1995), 126.
6. Ray Didinger, *Game Plans for Success* (Boston: Little, Brown & Company, 1995), 181.

Chapter 5   First You Feed the Troops

1. "Business Secrets of Tommy Lasorda," *Fortune*, July 3, 1989, 131.
2. Rick Newman, "Delta Takes Flight," *U.S. News and World Report*, May 20, 2007.
3. "Dinosaurs?" *Fortune*, May 3, 1993, 37.
4. "Ahead of Wall Street," *Wall Street Journal*, January 4, 2012.
5. "GM's Market Value Is Only $7 Billion—Half that of Avon," CNBC, June 26, 2008.
6. "UAW Contract Talks at a Glance," *Associated Press*, November 19, 2008.
7. "General Motors Loses $4.3 Billion, Says Profit Is Possible This Year," *Washington Post*, April 8, 2010.

Chapter 6   Tell 'Em the Truth

1. Rep. Barney Frank, House Financial Services Committee Hearing, September 10, 2003.

2. Alec Mattinson and Matt Cartmell, "Firms Fail to Reassure Employees Find an FD and YouGov Report," *PR Week*, June 3, 2009.
3. "Business Has a Job to Do: Rebuild Trust," *Fortune*, May 4, 2009.
4. Mark Zuckerberg, chief executive, *The Facebook Blog*, September 8, 2006.

Chapter 7   When Times Get Tough

1. "Hurricane Katrina Job Losses," *NPR*, October 7, 2005.
2. "I Can't Get No . . . Job Satisfaction, That Is," *The Conference Board*, January 2010.
3. "Inside Employees' Minds: Navigating the New Rules of Engagement," Mercer, July 2011.
4. Antonia Oprita, "A Third of U.K. Employees Unhappy in Their Jobs," CNBC, October 25, 2011.
5. William McKinley, Allen G. Schick, Carol M. Sanchez, "Organizational Downsizing: Constraining, Cloning, Learning," *Academy of Management Executive* 9, no. 3 (1995).
6. Peter Lynch Interview, *Worth*, June 1996, 89.
7. Jack Stack, "Mad about Layoffs," *INC* magazine, May 1996, 21.

Chapter 9   A Case for Some Useful Benefits

1. Company benefits page of google.com.
2. Paul Fronstin, "Sources of Health Insurance and Characteristics of the Uninsured," Employee Benefit Research Institute, March 2011.
3. "Income, Poverty, and Health Insurance Coverage in the United States," U.S. Census Bureau, 2009.
4. "Pay Matters: The Positive Economic Impacts of Paid Family Leave for Families, Businesses and the Public," Center for Women and Work, Rutgers, The State University of New Jersey, January 2012, 6.
5. Canada's Top 100 Employers, 2012.

Chapter 10   Empower This!

1. Henry Mintzberg, "Musings on Management," *Harvard Business Review*, July/August 1996.
2. GE Annual Reports, 1995–2000.

Chapter 11   Enabled Employees Are Incredibly Well Trained

1. "The 2011 State of the Industry," American Society for Training and Development.
2. Ibid.
3. "USAA's Battle Plan," *BusinessWeek*, February 18, 2010.
4. "2011 Training Top 125 Best Practices and Outstanding Initiatives," *Training*, January–February 2011, 98.

Chapter 12   Enabled Employees Are Tooled

1. "State: Sears Defrauds on Auto Repairs," *San Francisco Examiner*, June 11, 1992.
2. Frank Koller, *Spark: How Old-Fashioned Values Drive a Twenty-First Century Corporation* (New York: Public Affairs Books, 2010).
3. William L. McKnight, "Philosophy of Management," 1941.

Chapter 13   Enabled Employees Are Trusted

1. "At Work, Are You Trustworthy?" *Wall Street Journal*, September 20, 2009.
2. "Nordstrom Authorizes $800 Million Stock Buyback and Increased Dividend," Y-Charts, February 2012.
3. David Packard, *The HP Way* (New York: HarperBusiness, 1996), 136.
4. Ibid.

Chapter 14   When the Contented Cows Come Home
(Speculations on the Near Future)

1. Pat Riley, *The Winner Within* (New York: Putnam, 1993).
2. Frank Doyle, The Committee for Economic Development, 1996.

INDEX